THE BEST IN TENT CAMPING:

SMOKY MOUNTAINS

A Guide for Campers Who Hate RVs, Concrete Slabs, and Loud Portable Stereos

THE BEST IN TENT CAMPING:

SMOKY MOUNTAINS

A Guide for Campers Who Hate RVs, Concrete Slabs, and Loud Portable Stereos

Johnny Molloy

Printed in the United States of America
Published by Menasha Ridge Press
First edition, first printing

Library of Congress Cataloging-in-Publication Data

Molloy, Johnny, 1961-
The best in tent camping : Smoky Mountains : a guide for campers who hate RVs, concrete slabs, and loud portable stereos /
Johnny Molloy.—1st ed.
p. cm.
Includes bibliographical references.
ISBN 0-89732-233-9
1. Camp sites, facilities, etc.—Great Smoky Mountains (N.C. and Tenn.)—Guidebooks. 2. Camping—Great Smoky Mountains (N.C. and Tenn.)—Guidebooks. 3. Great Smoky Mountains (N.C. and Tenn.)—Guidebooks. I. Title.
GV191.42.G73M65 1996
796.54'0976889—dc21 97-9556
CIP

Cover design by Grant Tatum
Cover photo by Dennis Coello
Maps by Brian Taylor

Menasha Ridge Press
P.O. Box 43059
Birmingham, Alabama 35243

CONTENTS

South Carolina Campgrounds

Georgia Campgrounds

Appendices

MAP LEGEND

WHITE WOLF
Campground name and location

Table Rock
Other nearby campgrounds

NATIONAL FOREST | NATIONAL PARK
Public lands

N
0 1 2
MILES
Approximate scale

64
Interstate highways

40
U.S. highways

120 49
State roads

22
Other paved roads

Unpaved roads

4WD
Jeep roads

FS 80
U.S. Forest Service roads

Railroads

Asheville
City or town

Ward Lake
Ocean, lake, or bay

Swift Creek
River or stream

Political boundary

Bridge or tunnel

Cliff or outcropping

Falls or rapid

Food

Historical site

House or cabin

Lighthouse

Lodging

Marina or boat ramp

Mine or quarry

Museum

Observatory

ORV area

Park office

Picnic area

Spring

Stable or ranch

3312
Summit or lookout

This book is for Jill and Nelle Molloy,
two of a kind.

ACKNOWLEDGMENTS

I would like to thank the following people for their help in completing this book: Margaret Albrecht, Angie Bell, Laura Burgess, Deal Holcomb, Steve Grayson, Deborah Turpin, Bill Mai, Tom Rogers, Nancy McBee, Molly Burns, Tom Lauria, Francisco Meyer, Michael Molloy, and Karen Tate. A special thanks goes to David Zaczyk, Hunt Cochrane, and Kim Breasseale for lending their talents.

Along the way I met a lot of helpful public servants. I would like to acknowledge the contributions of the following: Georgia State Park personnel, Chattahoochee National Forest personnel, Sumter National Forest personnel, South Carolina State Park personnel, Cherokee National Forest personnel, Nantahala National Forest personnel, North Carolina State Park personnel, Pisgah National Forest personnel, Tennessee State Park personnel, and all the tent campers who shared their thoughts and a cup of coffee.

THE BEST IN TENT CAMPING:

SMOKY MOUNTAINS

A Guide for Campers Who Hate RVs, Concrete Slabs, and Loud Portable Stereos

PREFACE

Before there were cars, cable television, and computers, life moved at a much more manageable pace. Now, in the age of the Internet, folks just can't seem to find the time to be together. And when they do, the results can be disappointing. The traditional vacations to worn-out tourist traps minimize the companionship sought in such an outing.

A tent camping excursion is the answer to this quest for companionship. There's no dragging from attraction to attraction or fighting over where to eat. A tent camping trip can be a time of bonding on the trail and around the fire, where experiences and sights are shared. It is a chance to experience the unique loveliness of the out-of-doors and enjoy a little fun along the way.

As we enter the second millennium, camping allows time for introspection not found in this rush-rush world. To commune with nature is a rewarding experience for young and old alike. It is healthful for the mind and body to return to the land from which we came. Tent camping is a true vacation for all, that is, if you choose the right campground.

That is where this book can help. Once you've made the commitment to go tent camping, finding the right campground can make or break the adventure. Campgrounds range in character from roadside, RV-infested "cities" to secluded hideaways nestled deep in the bosom of the mountains.

In my Jeep, I coursed through Smoky Mountain country, searching for the best campgrounds throughout the mountains of Tennessee, North Carolina, South Carolina, and Georgia. I sought those nearest to a wilderness experience—those not overrun by RVs. Now it's up to you to glean your favorites from this book, get back to nature, and make some memories of your own.

—Johnny Molloy

INTRODUCTION

A Word about This Book and Smoky Mountain Camping

The *Southern Appalachians.* The very words give rise to images of misty, tree-topped mountains; clear, white-water streams; lush woodlands; and a biodiversity unmatched in the temperate climes. At the heart of the Southern Appalachians are the Smokies—the 500,000-acre master mountain chain containing the highest, wildest country remaining in the East. The Great Smoky Mountains National Park justifiably attracts millions of people per year. The allure of the Smokies often overshadows special areas adjacent to the park. Literally encircling the park are millions of acres of state park and national forest land that avails Smoky Mountain country to the public. This book covers not only the Smokies, but also the highlands of eastern Tennessee, western North Carolina, northern Georgia, and western South Carolina.

This is a region steeped in human and natural history. These mountains played a significant role in the formation and westward expansion of our country. Oftentimes, this expansion was at the expense of the Cherokee, who battled the settler and lost, but eventually managed to hold on to some of their ancestral lands. Aside from a few Civil War skirmishes, this land became a forgotten backwater, the land of "do-without." That was until logging interests discovered its magnificent forests and began to cut them down. Thankfully, some stands were left intact; the Smokies still contain some 125,000 acres of old-growth woods. After the harvest in the early 1900s, the Forest Service took over the fire-scarred and eroded lands, protecting and managing the area for commercial and recreational purposes: the multiple-use concept. Other special mountain places came under state protection, forming a nucleus of fine state parks.

A trip into the Southern Appalachians is like going from Georgia to Maine without all the driving. The elevation rise from 700 to 6,700 feet creates climate conditions like those ranging from Dixie to New England. Within those climate zones are habitats that foster plant and animal life found from Georgia to Maine. These conditions create the biodiversity that makes the Southern Appalachians special.

Generally speaking, spring takes six weeks to climb the mountains. Conversely, autumn descends the mountains six weeks earlier than in the surrounding lowlands. All of this adds to the biodiversity and makes for varying weather conditions to suit your whims as you seek the wildflowers of

spring, the lushness of summer, the colors of autumn, and the snows of winter. Luckily for us, there are plenty of campgrounds tucked away in Smoky Mountain country.

The rating system

Included in this book is a rating system for the Southern Appalachian's 50 best campgrounds. Certain campground attributes—beauty, site privacy, site spaciousness, quiet, security, and cleanliness/upkeep—are ranked using a star system. Five stars are ideal and one star is acceptable. This system will help you find the campground that has the attributes you desire.

Beauty

In the best campgrounds, the fluid shapes and elements of nature—flora, water, land, and sky—have melded to create locales that seem to have been made for tent camping. The best sites are so attractive you may be tempted not to leave your outdoor home. A little site work is OK to make the scenic area camper-friendly, but too many reminders of civilization eliminated many a campground from inclusion in this book.

Site privacy

A little understory goes a long way in making you feel comfortable once you've picked your site for the night. There is a trend of planting natural borders between campsites if the borders don't exist already. With some trees or brush to define the sites, everyone has their personal space. Then you can go about the pleasures of tent camping without keeping up with the Joneses at the next site over—or them with you.

Site spaciousness

This attribute can be very important depending on how much of a gearhead you are and the size of your group. Campers with family-style tents need a large flat spot on which to pitch their tent and still get to the ice chest to prepare foods, all the while not getting burned near the fire ring. Gearheads need

adequate space to show off all their stuff to neighbors strolling by. I just want enough room to keep my bedroom, kitchen, and den separate.

Quiet
The music of the mountains—singing birds, rushing streams, wind rattling leaves, and raindrops pattering the forest floor—includes the kind of noises tent campers associate with being in the Southern Appalachians. In concert, they camouflage the sounds you don't want to hear—autos coming and going, loud neighbors, and the like.

Security
Campground security is relative. A remote campground with no civilization nearby is relatively safe, but don't tempt potential thieves by leaving your valuables out for all to see. Use common sense and go with your instinct. Campground hosts are wonderful to have around, and state parks with locked gates at night are ideal for security. Get to know your neighbors and develop a buddy system to watch each other's belongings when possible.

Cleanliness/upkeep
I'm a stickler for this one. Nothing will sabotage a scenic campground like trash. Most of the campgrounds in this book are clean. More rustic campgrounds, my favorites, usually receive less maintenance. Busy weekends and holidays will show their effects. But don't let a little litter spoil your good time. Help clean up and think of it as doing your part for our natural environment.

Helpful hints
To make the most of your camping trip, call ahead wherever possible. If going to a state park, call for an informative brochure before you set out; this way you can familiarize yourself with the area. Once there, ask questions. Most stewards of the land are proud of their piece of terra firma and are honored you came for a visit and want you to have the best time possible.

If traveling to a national forest, call ahead and order a map of the forest you plan to enter. Not only will this make it that much easier to reach your destination, but nearby hikes, scenic drives, waterfalls, and landmarks will be easier to find. More and more national forests are erecting Visitor Centers in addition to Ranger Stations. Call or visit and ask questions. And when ordering maps, also ask for any additional literature about the area in which you are interested.

In writing this book I had the pleasure of meeting many friendly, helpful people: local residents who were proud of their Southern mountains; state park and national forest employees who endured my endless barrage of questions; and many campers who shared a cup of coffee and piece of their time. They already know what a lovely place this is. And as the splendor of the Southern Appalachians becomes more recognized, these mountain lands become that much more precious. Enjoy them, protect them, and use them wisely.

TENNESSEE CAMPGROUNDS

ABRAMS CREEK CAMPGROUND

Townsend, Tennessee

Campers don't just stumble into this well-kept secret, hidden at the end of a gravel road off a meandering valley road. But those who find it make it worth their time. Located at the extreme western edge of the Smokies, Abrams Creek Campground may be off the beaten tourist path, but nearby there are plenty of footpaths, as well as a few other activities. Located in a wooded flat along a tranquil section of Abrams Creek, this intimate campground provides a relaxing setting not found in most national park campgrounds. The 16 sites are usually filled only on weekends and holidays. The place seems nearly deserted on lazy summer weekdays. About half the sites are creekside, but all are well shaded.

If relaxing under a towering white pine in a quiet woodland beside a cool mountain stream is your pleasure, this is the campground for you. This place exudes an atmosphere of escape from civilization. Since it is in the park's lowlands, this campground can be fairly warm, if not downright hot, in the summer. But no matter how hot it gets during the day, you can always expect it to cool down in the evening. A water fountain and cold running water, situated in the middle of the campground, are there to slake your thirst and satisfy your water needs.

The creek and campground were named after Old Abram, Cherokee chief of the

CAMPGROUND RATINGS

Beauty:	★★★★★
Site privacy:	★★★
Site spaciousness:	★★★★
Quiet:	★★★★★
Security:	★★★★
Cleanliness/upkeep:	★★★★★

Abrams Creek Campground offers national park–level beauty and recreational opportunities in an off-the-beaten-path atmosphere.

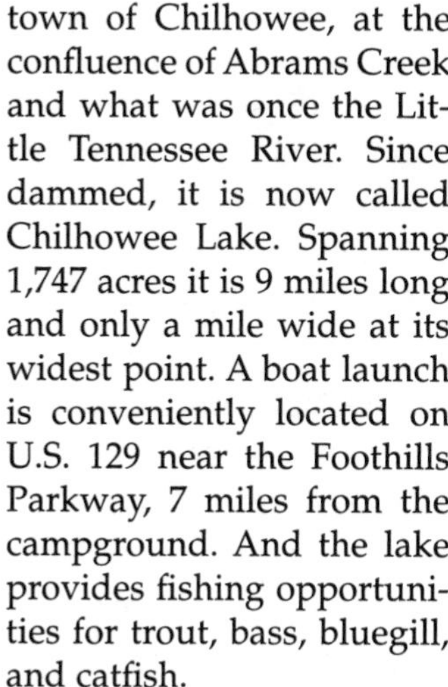

town of Chilhowee, at the confluence of Abrams Creek and what was once the Little Tennessee River. Since dammed, it is now called Chilhowee Lake. Spanning 1,747 acres it is 9 miles long and only a mile wide at its widest point. A boat launch is conveniently located on U.S. 129 near the Foothills Parkway, 7 miles from the campground. And the lake provides fishing opportunities for trout, bass, bluegill, and catfish.

Don't let the low elevation of the campground make you underestimate the ruggedness of this country. Between the sharp, wooded ridges flow twisting streams overgrown with rhododendron, where black bear, deer, and other fauna forage for their livelihood. The area recently got a little wilder, as the park service acquired 400 critical acres near the park border downstream from the campground. Despite its wildness, a fine trail system offers pleasant hiking.

And for those in a walking frame of mind, the Cooper Road Trail conveniently starts at the back of the campground. Once on the Cooper Road Trail, you can make a 7.5-mile loop hike. This will give you a good taste of the pine-oak woods within this area of the park. Using a combination of the Little Bottoms, Hannah Mountain, and Rabbit Creek trails, you will see the Abrams Creek Gorge and a couple of old homesites while passing three backcountry campsites. The loop ends at the Abrams Creek Ranger Station near the campground. Another hike, historical in nature, takes you to the old Buchannan Cemetery using a combination of the Cooper Road and Cane Creek trails. This cemetery underscores the fact that people once lived in the Smokies, and many locals in the nearby Happy Valley still feel a special kinship for their Tennessee mountain homes.

If you are feeling really aggressive, climb Pine Mountain. It's 2 miles up the Rabbit Creek Trail, starting near the Ranger Station. Cross Abrams Creek on a footlog with a handrail, pass the old homesite on your left, then start climbing. A semicircle of stones marks the high point on the trail, where Chilhowee Mountain can be seen to the north. On the way down, see if you can spot the Ranger Station between the trees.

A rewarding hike is the 10-mile round-trip walk to Abrams Falls, a popular destination, but few make the trip from Abrams Campground. After a short mile on Cooper Road, turn on the Little Bottoms Trail and continue to follow Abrams Creek to the falls. The wide rush of Abrams Creek drops into a large plunge pool, where hot hikers often take a dip in the cool mountain water. In late spring this route is brightened by the pink and white blooms of the ubiquitous mountain laurel.

Downstream, a long quiet pool abuts the campground, enticing its share of swimmers and anglers alike. Rainbow trout inhabit these waters, and since it's the park's lowlands, this is one of the few park streams that also include feisty rock bass and their larger cousin, the smallmouth bass. A Tennessee state fishing license is required, but the license allows anglers to fish park waters in both Tennessee and North Carolina.

If you need supplies, head back out to U.S. 129, turn right, and drive 5 miles to the old-time Tallassee General Store. Established in 1933 and complete with a potbellied stove, it offers both modern camping supplies and old-fashioned dry goods. Run by Charlie Lunsford, it also serves as the post office and gossip center for the surrounding community.

KEY INFORMATION

Abrams Creek Campground
6537 Abrams Creek Road
Tallassee, TN 37878

Operated by: Great Smoky Mountains National Park

Information: (423) 436-1228

Open: May to October

Individual sites: 16

Each site has: Picnic table, fire pit, lantern post

Site assignment: First come, first served; no reservations

Registration: Self-registration on site

Facilities: Flush toilets, cold running water

Parking: At individual sites

Fee: $6 per night

Elevation: 1,125 feet

Restrictions:

Pets—On leash only

Fires—In fire pits only

Alcoholic beverages—At campsite only

Vehicles—Small trailers up to 12 feet; no RV hookups

Other—7-day stay limit

To get there, from Townsend, Tennessee, drive north on U.S. 321. Turn left off the Foothills Parkway at Chilhowee Lake onto U.S. 129. Head south .5 mile to Happy Valley Road. Turn left on Happy Valley Road, following it 6 miles to Abrams Creek Road. Turn right on Abrams Creek Road and drive 1 mile to the campground, passing the Ranger Station on your left.

BANDY CREEK CAMPGROUND

Oneida, Tennessee

The National Park Service is catching on quite nicely. It realizes there are two divergent groups that use campgrounds: tent campers and RVers. Here at Bandy Creek Campground, the Park Service has designated a tents-only loop that places compatible groups together. It's a good thing, because a recommended campground completes the superlative outdoor package that is the Big South Fork.

Protected since 1974, the Big South Fork features wild rivers, steep gorges, thick forests, and human history set atop the Cumberland Plateau. A well-developed trail system with trails leaving directly from the campground makes exploring the Big South Fork easy. There are also mountain biking, canoeing, fishing, and rafting opportunities.

Bandy Creek Campground is a large complex with a total of four camping loops. A recreation area and the park's Visitor Center are nearby. Loop A is the only loop available to tent campers exclusively. It veers off to the left after the campground registration booth and is separated from the rest of the campground.

The campground is generally wooded. A few sites back up against a field and the recreation complex, which includes a swimming pool and a playground for young campers. Since Bandy Creek is atop the plateau, the forest is mixed hardwood with oaks, tulip trees, and Virginia pine.

CAMPGROUND RATINGS

Beauty: ★★★
Site privacy: ★★★
Site spaciousness: ★★★★
Quiet: ★★★
Security: ★★★★
Cleanliness/upkeep: ★★★★★

Bandy Creek Campground lies at the heart of the 100,000-acre Big South Fork National River and Recreation Area.

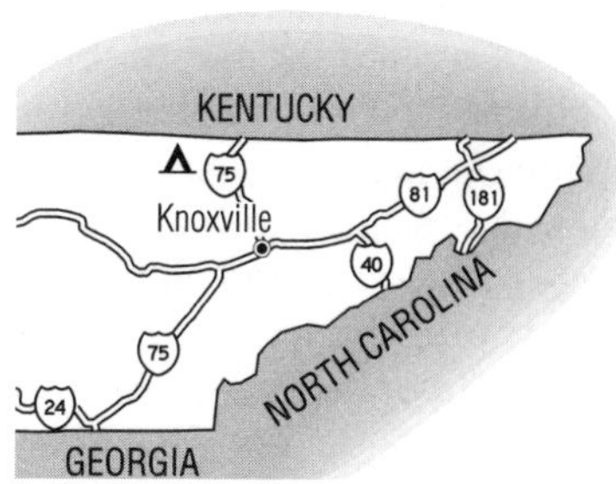

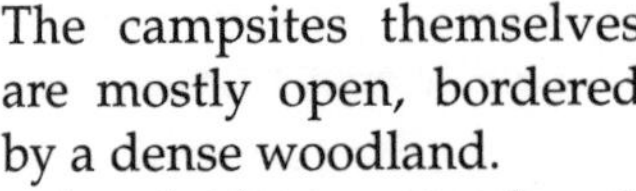

The campsites themselves are mostly open, bordered by a dense woodland.

A mini-loop extends off Loop A and contains four out-of-the-way sites. Beyond the first mini-loop, campsites with paved parking areas extend on either side of the road as it rises slightly, passing one of the two most complete washhouses I've ever encountered. The buildings are designed in the architecture of the locality and have a water fountain, piped water, flush toilets, showers, and even a two-basin sink for washing dishes! Farther on, the road divides and arrives at one of two bad sites in the campground: site #32 is adjacent to the water tower; site #2 backs against the swimming pool.

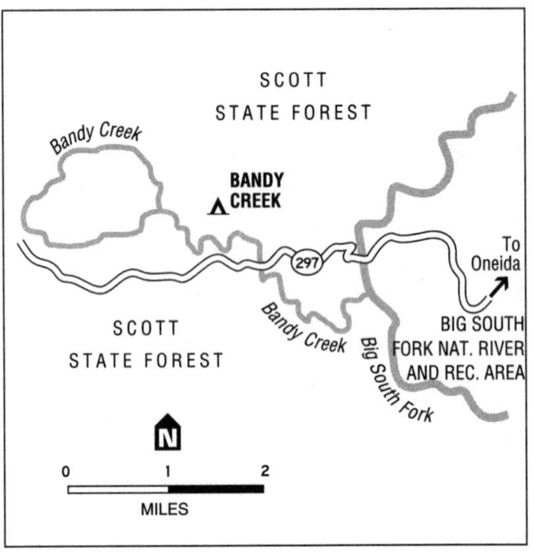

As Loop A swings around, another mini-loop veers off. It contains seven wooded sites that are the most private in the campground. The main road passes the second washhouse. Three other water pumps are dispersed among the 49 well-kept sites.

The rest of the campground contains 96 sites. Only Loop D, with 52 sites, is open to both tents and RVs during the winter. The pool is open from June to Labor Day, but the rest of this place is ready to be explored year-round.

Hiking is very popular. Why not? Trails lace the immediate area. The John Litton/General Slavens Loop traverses 6 miles of the surrounding countryside. It descends to the valley where the John Litton Farm stands, passes a large rock house, and climbs back up to the campground via Fall Branch Falls. If you prefer a trail with more human and natural history, take the Oscar Blevins Loop. It is a moderate, 3.6-mile loop that passes the Blevins Farm, some large trees, and more of the steep bluffs that characterize the Cumberland Plateau. Another hiking option is the easy Bandy Creek Campground loop. It is a short, 1.3-mile family hike that offers a good introduction to the area. Want more trails? Stop by the Visitor Center, and they can point you in the right direction.

If you don't feel like walking, ride a horse. The nearby Bandy Creek Stables offer guided rides for a fee.

Water enthusiasts should drive the short distance to Leatherwood Ford and the Big South Fork for recreation. There the river flows through a scenic gorge with steep cliffs soaring to the sky. Exciting rapids and decent fishing can be found both upstream and down. Check the Visitor Center for river conditions. I have used and can recommend Mark Liming of Backwoods Adventures for canoe rental and shuttle service. His phone number is (423) 569-9573. He also rents mountain bikes for pedaling down many of the paths and old roads that crisscross the area. Again, check with the Visitor Center for the best trails.

It is evident you won't be spending much time relaxing at the campground. There is simply too much to see and do. Come see the Big South Fork and you'll have spent your time well.

To get there, from Oneida take TN 297 west for 14 miles. Bandy Creek Campground will be on your right.

KEY INFORMATION

Bandy Creek Campground
Route 3, Box 401
Oneida, TN 37841

Operated by: National Park Service

Information: (423) 569-9778

Open: March 15 to October 31; limited sites year-round

Individual sites: 49, tents only

Each site has: Tent pad, fire grate, picnic table, lantern post

Site assignment: First come, first served; no reservations

Registration: Self-registration on site

Facilities: Piped water, flush toilets, hot showers, pay phone

Parking: At campsites only

Fee: $12 per night

Elevation: 1,500 feet

Restrictions:

Pets—On a six-foot leash only

Fires—In fire grates only

Alcoholic beverages—At campsites only

Vehicles—Maximum 2 vehicles per site

Other—14-day stay limit

CHILHOWEE CAMPGROUND

Cleveland, Tennessee

The Chilhowee experience starts on the road to the campground. Forest Service Road 77 is a Forest Service–designated scenic byway that climbs 7 miles to the campground. Don't rush the trip—pull off at one of the cleared overlooks and enjoy the view of Parksville Lake below while mountains and valleys undulate in the distance. Once you've made the pull to the top and seen the campground, it's the nearby activities that may keep you from coming down for a while.

This mountaintop campground is a cool retreat during hot summer days. It is popular with families who return year after year. Chilhowee fills up on weekends and holidays. Tent camping is the norm here; the steep drive up the mountain discourages most RVs and trailers.

The campground itself spreads into three distinct areas. Loops A and B are the oldest and highest, built in the 1930s by the Civilian Conservation Corps. They are nestled in a dip on the mountain beneath a hardwood forest. Water spigots are well placed and accessible to all campers. Two comfort stations with flush toilets are available for each sex, but only Loop B has showers. A campground host keeps the area clean, safe, and secure.

Loops C, D, E, and F are newer and more spacious. They are placed where the mountain terrain allows and have more ground

CAMPGROUND RATINGS

Beauty: ★★★★
Site privacy: ★★★
Site spaciousness: ★★★★
Quiet: ★★★
Security: ★★★★★
Cleanliness/upkeep: ★★★★★

Chilhowee is a mountaintop campground with plenty of activities to keep campers busy and happy.

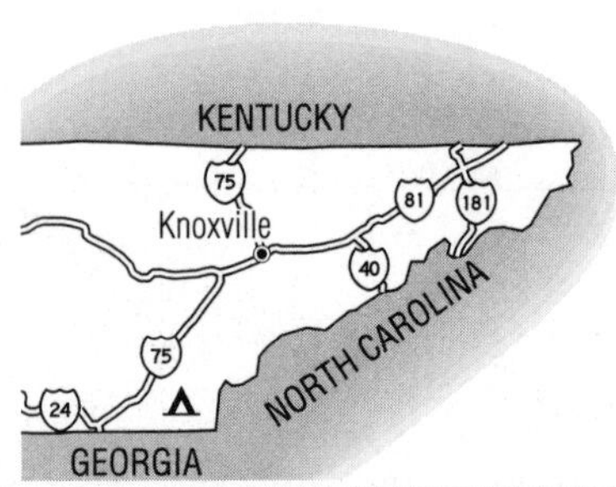

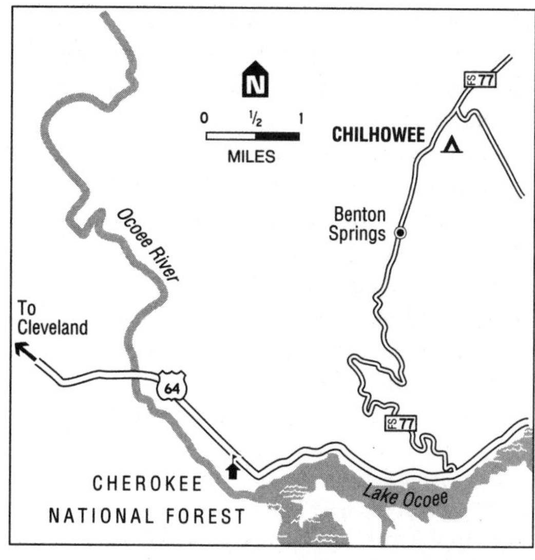

cover for privacy beneath the piney woods. Two comfort stations serve the four loops, but only Loop F has showers. Water is easily accessible in these loops.

The third area is for overflow camping and is located in an open, grassy field ringed by woods. It offers one comfort station, but no shower, for the 23 overflow sites. There is one water source here. The sites are near one another, which makes this arrangement neither spacious nor private, but campers make the most of it because of the recreational opportunities up here.

Want to take a hike? You won't have to go far from your campsite. The Azalea Trail begins in Loop F; it climbs the ridge above the campground and then makes a 2-mile loop back to the campground. Or keep going on the Clear Creek Trail to the north rim of the Rock Creek Gorge Scenic Area. Benton Falls Trail starts near Lake McCamy. It travels 1.6 miles and ends at the 65-foot falls. Be careful, it gets steep toward the end. Bicyclists can stretch their legs, too. Pedal the Red Leaf Trail to Benton Falls or ride the Arbutus Trail. If you're quiet, you might see some wildlife. All trails are open to both bikers and hikers.

If all that exercise gets you steamed up, take a dip in three-acre Lake McCamy. A swimming beach lies at the north end where sunbathers alternately lie in the sun and cool off in the water. Anglers can try to catch bream and bass from the shore, or they can toss a line from a small boat as long as it's nonmotorized.

Off the mountain along U.S. 64 is the famed Ocoee River. For years the water was diverted from the streambed to an old wooden flume for power purposes. When the flume began to leak, the water was again let loose on the Ocoee riverbed. Paddling enthusiasts realized the long lost rapids would be a wonderful challenge in a canoe, kayak, or raft, and the new recreational opportunity has been an economic boon to the area ever since. Paddlers come from all over the world to test the waters. The upper Ocoee was the site of the 1996 Olympic white-water events. Outfitters await to guide you down the crashing white water in a hair-raising raft ride.

Also along U.S. 64 you'll find the Scenic Spur Trail, a hiking-only venture into the heart of the Rock Creek Gorge Scenic Area. Walk slowly up the 1.7-mile footpath and see the effects of water, time, and the elements on the land. With all there is to do, remember you have a campground to attend in the evenings.

To get there, take U.S. 64 east from Cleveland for 12 miles. Just past the Ocoee District Ranger Station turn left on FS 77 for 7 miles. Chilhowee Campground will be on your right.

KEY INFORMATION

Chilhowee Campground
Route 1, Box 348D
Benton, TN 37307

Operated by: U.S. Forest Service

Information: (423) 338-5201

Open: April 1 to November 9

Individual sites: 88

Each site has: Picnic table, grill, lantern post

Site assignment: 48 sites are first come, first served; 40 sites are reservation only

Registration: Self-registration on site for 48 sites; otherwise, call (800) 280-CAMP; reservations must be made at least 10 days in advance and are accepted as early as 180 days in advance

Facilities: Cold showers, flush toilets, drinking water

Parking: At campsites only

Fee: $8 per night

Elevation: 2,600 feet

Restrictions:

Pets—On leash at all times

Fires—In fire grates only

Alcoholic beverages—Prohibited

Vehicles—None

Other—5 persons per campsite; 14-day stay limit

COSBY CAMPGROUND

Gatlinburg, Tennessee

Set on a slight incline in what once was pioneer farmland, this attractive, terraced campground is surrounded by mountains on three sides. The large camping area is situated between the confluence of Rock Creek and Cosby Creek. During my trips to the area, I have rarely seen this campground crowded, while other large Smokies campgrounds can be overflowing, cramped, and noisy. Several loops expand the campground, and bathrooms are conveniently located throughout the site. A small store, specializing in campers' needs, is located at the turn off TN 32.

Now beautifully reforested, this area is rich in Smoky Mountain history. Cosby was one of the most heavily settled areas in the Smokies before Uncle Sam began buying up land for a national park in the East. The farmland was marginal anyway, so, in order to supplement their income, Cosby residents set up moonshine stills in the remote hollows of this rugged country. As a result, Cosby became known as the "moonshine capital of the world."

In remote, brush-choked hollows along little streamlets, "blockaders"—as the moonshiners were known—established stills. Before too long they had clear whiskey, "mountain dew," ready for consumption. Government agents, known as "revenuers" and determined to stop the production and sale of "corn likker," battled the moonshiners throughout the

CAMPGROUND RATINGS

Beauty:	★★★★★
Site privacy:	★★★★
Site spaciousness:	★★★★★
Quiet:	★★★★
Security:	★★★★
Cleanliness:	★★★★★

Located off the principal tourist circuit, this cool, wooded campground makes an ideal base for exploring the virgin forests and high country of the Cosby/Greenbriar area.

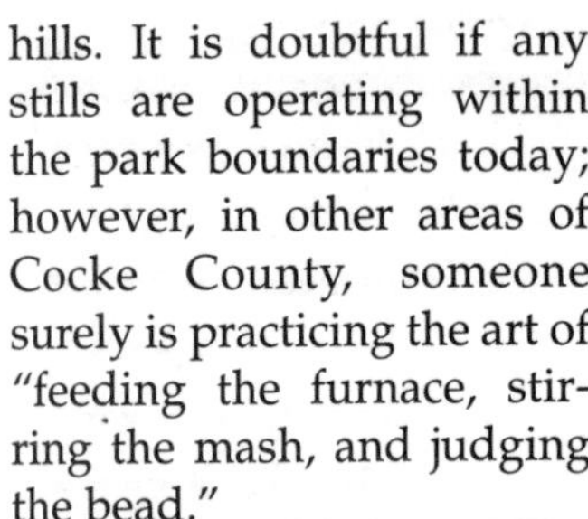

hills. It is doubtful if any stills are operating within the park boundaries today; however, in other areas of Cocke County, someone surely is practicing the art of "feeding the furnace, stirring the mash, and judging the bead."

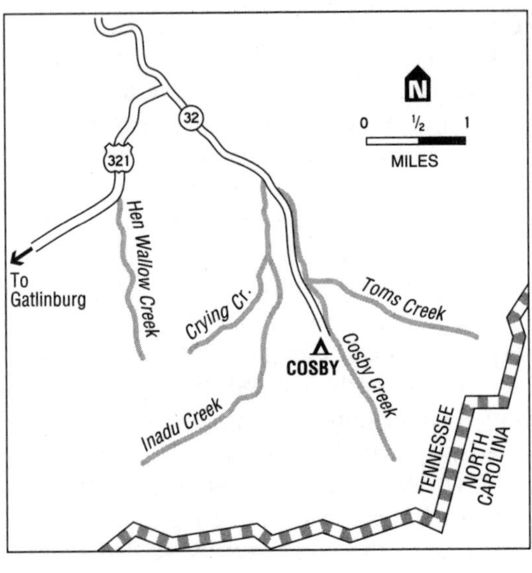

Its past is what makes Cosby so interesting. Trails split off in every direction, allowing campers to explore the human and natural history of this area. Follow the Lower Mount Cammerer Trail 1.5 miles to Sutton Ridge Overlook. On the way to the overlook watch for signs of homesteaders from bygone days: rock walls, springs, and old chimneys. At the overlook, you'll get a good lay of the land: Gabes Mountain to your east, the main crest of the Smokies to your south, the Cosby Valley below, and East Tennessee on the horizon.

Another hiking option is the Gabes Mountain Trail. Along its 6-mile length, this trail passes picturesque Henwallow Falls and meanders through huge, old-growth hemlock and tulip trees and scattered, old homesites. Turn around at the Sugar Cove backcountry campsite.

Don't forget to explore nearby Greenbriar. The 4-mile Ramsay Cascades Trail traverses virgin forest and ends at a picturesque waterfall that showers hikers with a fine mist. The Brushy Mountain Trail winds its way through several vegetation zones to an impressive view of the looming mass of Mount LeConte above and Gatlinburg below. Grapeyard Ridge Trail is the area's most historical and secluded hike. Walk old country paths along Rhododendron Creek and count the homesites amid fields just now being obscured by the forest. At 3 miles, just before the Injun Creek backcountry campsite, look for the old tractor that made its last turn in these Smoky Mountains.

The crown jewel hike from Cosby is the 6-mile hike to the restored Mount Cammerer fire tower. Built on a rock outcrop, it was formerly called White Rock by Tennesseans and Sharp Top by Carolinians. It has since been renamed Mount Cammerer, after Arno B. Cammerer, former director of the National Park Service. Restored by a philanthropic outfit called "Friends of the Smokies," the squat, wood and stone tower was originally built by the Depression-era Civilian Conservation Corps. The 360-degree view is well worth the climb. To the north is the Cosby Valley and the rock cut of I-40. Mount Sterling and its fire tower are to the south. The main crest of the Smokies stands to the west, and a wave of mountains fades off into the eastern horizon.

Cosby Campground is a winner. Where else can you set up your tent in the middle of history? In the summer, naturalist programs in the campground amphitheater offer campers a chance to learn more about the area from rangers and other park personnel. The campground's size allows campers to set up near or away from others to achieve their perfect degree of solitude. If you are in the mood for company, though, the tourist mecca of Gatlinburg is nearby. Attractions range from the visual (Elvis Museum, wax museums, and musical revues) to the gastronomical (fudge shops, taffy shops, breakfast buffets, and plenty of fine dining). Souvenir shops abound with coonskin caps, stuffed black bears, and ceramic chickens. Don't forget to have your picture taken in the old-time pioneer garb at the numerous photo shops. It really is a fun place to stroll and people-watch.

KEY INFORMATION

Cosby Campground
127 Cosby Park Road
Cosby, TN 37722

Operated by: Great Smoky Mountains National Park

Information: (423) 436-1228

Open: May to October

Individual sites: 175

Each site has: Picnic table, fire pit, lantern post

Site assignment: First come, first served; no reservations

Registration: At the hut at the campground's entrance

Facilities: Flush toilets, cold running water

Parking: At individual sites

Fee: $8 per night

Elevation: 2,459 feet

Restrictions:

Pets—On leash only

Fires—In fire pits

Alcoholic beverages—At campsites only

Vehicles—None

Other—7-day stay limit

To get there, from Gatlinburg take U.S. 321 east until it comes to a T intersection with TN 32. Follow TN 32 a little over a mile, turning right into the signed Cosby section of the park. After 2.1 miles, arrive at the campground registration hut. The campground is just beyond the hut.

DENNIS COVE CAMPGROUND

Hampton, Tennessee

If you feel your taxes are too high, come stay at Dennis Cove Campground. You can camp here for free and enjoy the delightful national forest that surrounds the fine campground. It can be busy on weekends, but no busier than pay campgrounds. There are fishing and hiking opportunities at Dennis Cove that will help you recoup some of the investment you made in these public lands. They are, after all, your lands to enjoy.

The intimate campground is set in a small flat alongside Laurel Fork. A steep, sloped ridge and thickly wooded creek hem in the campground. There is no mistake, you are deep in the bosom of the Southern Appalachians. The bellwether of eastern mountain beauty, the Appalachian Trail, runs near here and is easily accessible from the campground itself.

As you pull into the campground from Forest Service Road 50, a small, grassy glade provides sunlight in this deeply forested cove. This area was timbered in the 1920s and has recovered nicely. A teardrop-shaped loop holds 13 of the 16 campsites. The first two sites abut the glade. Two other sites lie inside the loop, which has a grassy area of its own. The next three sites on the outside of the loop are heavily shaded beneath hemlock trees. Then the loop swings around to the four most popular sites. They are situated alongside gurgling Laurel Fork. The

CAMPGROUND RATINGS

Beauty: ★★★★
Site privacy: ★★★
Site spaciousness: ★★★★
Quiet: ★★★★
Security: ★★★
Cleanliness/upkeep: ★★★★

Camping is free at Dennis Cove, where recreational opportunities abound at every turn.

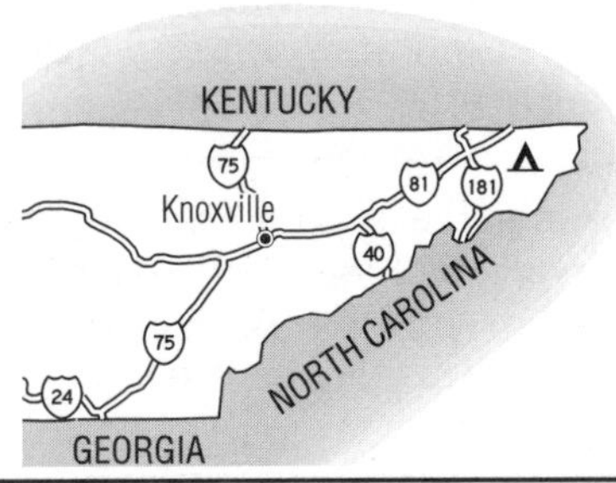

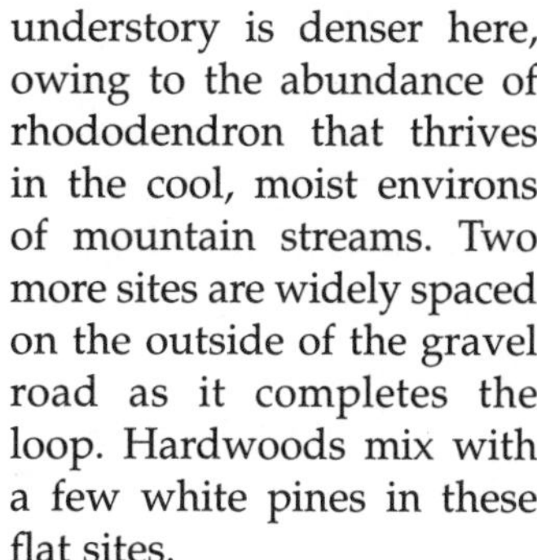

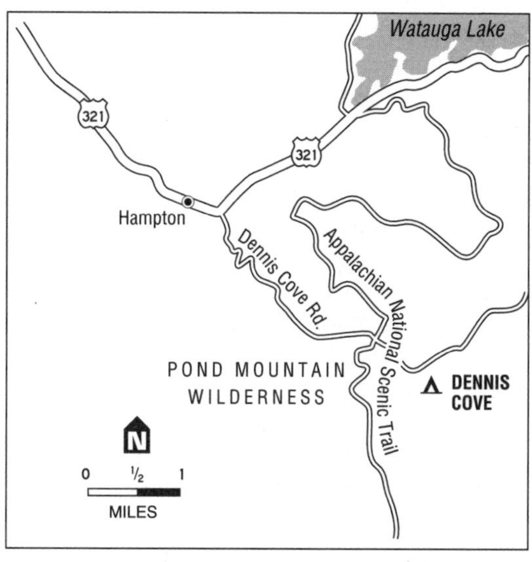

understory is denser here, owing to the abundance of rhododendron that thrives in the cool, moist environs of mountain streams. Two more sites are widely spaced on the outside of the gravel road as it completes the loop. Hardwoods mix with a few white pines in these flat sites.

Three other sites lie across the gravel road leading to the loop. These sites, large by any campground standard, are carved out of the steep hill bordering Dennis Cove. Each site is separated by woodland. If it has been raining lately, as it often does in the mountains, these spots are your best bet for a high and dry campsite.

Moss grows on the stones scattered about the area. It is evident this campground has been around a long time; however, it receives periodic revamping. During my visit, the loop road had been freshly graveled and the fire rings rebuilt.

Three water spigots are evenly dispersed about the loop. Just turn the handle and the water's yours. A small comfort station, with one flush toilet for each sex, is 100 feet off the loop away from the campground entrance.

Explore the environs after you've set up camp. The waterfall enthusiast has three destinations within walking distance. Walk back toward Hampton half a mile and soon you'll see a creek coming in on the left. Follow the old, .8-mile trail made by Dennis Cove campers up to Coon Den Falls. This trail will be the Appalachian Trail after relocation efforts are completed. If you continue beyond the falls, you can access the AT. Turn left and come to Whiterock Lookout Tower in another mile.

Back down a little farther on FS 50 toward Hampton you'll find more Appalachian Trail. Leave FS 50 and follow the old railroad grade into the Laurel Fork Gorge and the Pond Mountain Wilderness. Rock outcrops and a riverine environment lead you to Laurel Falls. If you keep going, you'll end up in Maine.

Forest Trail #39 leaves from the campground and follows Laurel Fork into the high country. This trail crosses Laurel Fork several times. It leads to Laurel Falls upstream. This trail is popular with fishermen, who match wits with the secretive brown trout that inhabit Laurel Fork. Forest Trails #36 and #38 connect to the AT near Whiterock for loop-hiking possibilities.

The recreational opportunities at Dennis Cove are limited only by your desire. Your only investment is time. The camping is free. The 6,000-acre Pond Mountain Wilderness is close by, as is mountain-rimmed Watauga Lake.

To get there, from Hampton drive north on U.S. 321 for .8 mile. Watch carefully for the sign with the picture of a tent on it on the road's right. Turn right there. It's the unmarked Dennis Cove Road. Climb away from Hampton for 3.9 twisting, turning miles. Dennis Cove Campground will be on your right.

KEY INFORMATION

Dennis Cove Campground
1205 North Main Street
Erwin, TN 37650

Operated by: U.S. Forest Service

Information: (423) 743-4452

Open: May 1 to October 7

Individual sites: 16

Each site has: Tent pad, fire ring, lantern post, picnic table

Site assignment: First come, first served; no reservations

Registration: Not necessary

Facilities: Flush toilets, piped water

Parking: At campsites only

Fee: None

Elevation: 2,600 feet

Restrictions:

Pets—On 6-foot leash only

Fires—In fire rings only

Alcoholic beverages—Prohibited

Vehicles—None

Other—14-day stay limit

FOSTER FALLS STATE PARK

Tracy City, Tennessee

The south end of the Cumberland Plateau has some of the wildest, roughest country in Tennessee. Sheer bluffs border deep gulfs—what natives call gorges. In these gorges flow wild streams strewn with rock gardens hosting a variety of vegetation. Intermingled within this is a human history of logging and mining that has given way to the nonextractive use of nature: ecotourism.

Foster Falls, formerly operated by the Tennessee Valley Authority, has been taken over by Tennessee State Parks. It offers a safe and appealing base for your camping experience in the South Cumberlands. The campground is situated on a level, wooded tract near Foster Falls. It features the classic loop design, only the loop is so large it seems to engulf the 26 sites spread along it. Hardwoods give way to pines as you head toward the forested back of the loop. An interesting tree in the campground is the umbrella magnolia. Its leaves can reach two feet in length, causing its limbs to sag during the summer. Look for the tree along the campground entrance road and among sites 1–10.

The spindly, second-growth tree trunks form a light understory, but the campsites are so diffused that site privacy isn't compromised. The understory actually lends a parklike atmosphere to the campground. Foster Falls has some of the most spacious campsites I've ever seen. The

CAMPGROUND RATINGS

Beauty:	★★★
Site privacy:	★★★
Site spaciousness:	★★★★★
Quiet:	★★★
Security:	★★★★★
Cleanliness/upkeep:	★★★★

Foster Falls State Park can be your headquarters for exploring the South Cumberland Recreation Area.

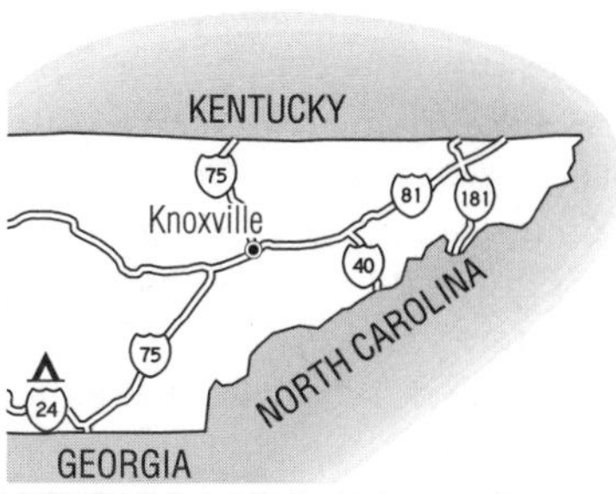

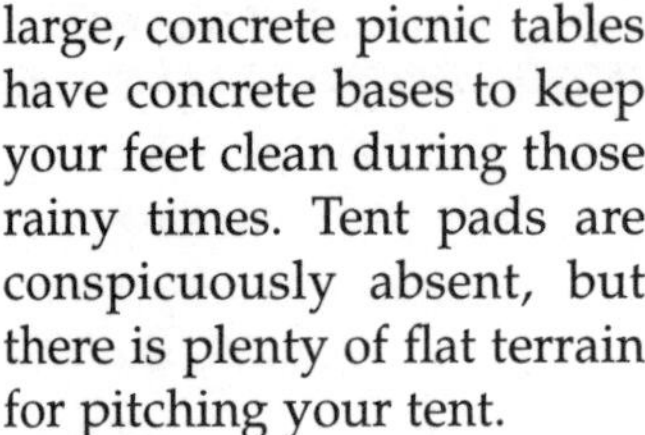

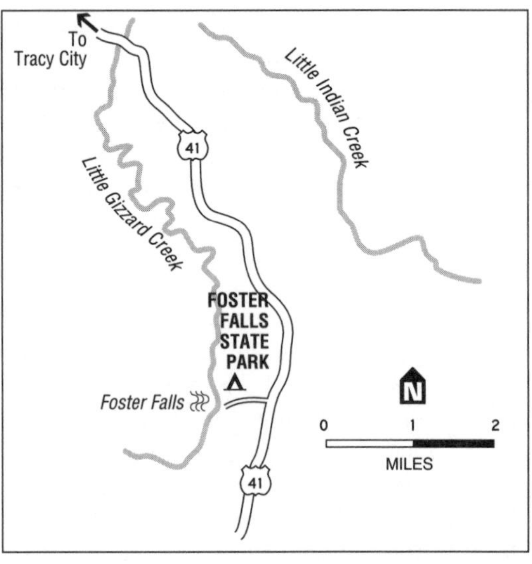

large, concrete picnic tables have concrete bases to keep your feet clean during those rainy times. Tent pads are conspicuously absent, but there is plenty of flat terrain for pitching your tent.

The three water spigots are handy to all campsites, but the comfort station is located on one side of the loop, making a midnight bathroom run a little long for those distant campers. However, this campground is rarely full, so you should be able to secure a site near the comfort station if you prefer a shorter trip. Quite often, your camping companions will be rock climbers, for Foster Falls has quietly emerged as the premier rock-climbing area in the Southeast.

A park manager lives on site across from the campground entrance for your security and the security of your gear while you check out the rest of the South Cumberland Recreation Area. The SCRA has eight different units, totaling over 12,000 acres, ready for you to enjoy.

For starters, a connector trail leaves the campground to Foster Falls. Here, you can take the short loop trail that leads to the base of 120-foot Foster Falls or intersect the south end of the Fiery Gizzard Trail and see Foster Falls from the top looking down. If you take the Fiery Gizzard Trail, you will be rewarded with views into Little Gizzard and Fiery Gizzard gulfs. Trail signs point out the rock bluffs where rock climbers ply their trade. The first 2.5 miles offer many vistas and small waterfalls where side creeks plunge into the gorge below. My favorite view is from the Laurel Creek Gorge Overlook, where rock bluffs on the left meld into forested drop-offs beyond, contrasting with the flat plateau in the background.

Other must-sees in the South Cumberlands are Grundy Forest, Grundy Lakes, Savage Gulf, and the Great Stone Door. Administrators at Foster Falls will direct you to all the sights. Grundy Forest contains about 4 miles of the most feature-packed hiking you can ask for: waterfalls, rock houses, old trees, old mines, and strange rock formations. Just remember to watch where you walk, as the trails can be rough.

Grundy Lakes State Park is on the National Historic Register. Once the site of mining activity, this area has seen prison labor, revolts, and the cooling down of the infamous Lone Rock coke ovens. The Lone Rock Trail will lead you to all the interesting sites.

At Savage Gulf State Natural Area, three gorges converge to form a giant crow's foot. An extensive trail system connects the cliffs, waterfalls, sinkholes, and historic sites of the area. The Great Stone Door is a 10-by-100-foot crack in the Big Creek Gorge that was used by Indians who traversed Savage Gulf.

The campground at Foster Falls State Park is pleasant enough to stay a week or more, and that's about how long you'll need to get a good taste of the South Cumberland Recreation Area.

To get there, from Tracy City take U.S. 41 south for 8 miles and turn right at the sign for Foster Falls. The campground will be .3 mile on your left.

KEY INFORMATION

Foster Falls State Park
Route 1, Box 2196
Monteagle, TN 37356

Operated by: Tennessee State Parks

Information: (615) 924-2980

Open: April 15 to October 15

Individual sites: 26

Each site has: Fire grate, picnic table, lantern post

Site assignment: First come, first served; no reservations

Registration: Ranger will come by and register you

Facilities: Piped water, flush toilets

Parking: At campsites only

Fee: $11 per night

Elevation: 1,750 feet

Restrictions:

Pets—On a 6-foot leash only

Fires—In fire grates only

Alcoholic beverages—Prohibited

Vehicles—None

Other—14-day stay limit

FROZEN HEAD STATE PARK

Oak Ridge, Tennessee

CAMPGROUND RATINGS

Beauty:	★★★★★
Site privacy:	★★★
Site spaciousness:	★★★★
Quiet:	★★★★★
Security:	★★★★★
Cleanliness/upkeep:	★★★★★

Stay at Frozen Head and explore the waterfalls, rock shelters, and mountaintop caprocks of the rugged Cumberland Mountains.

Frozen Head is a little-known jewel of a state park tucked away in the Cumberland Mountains, a mountain range west of the Smokies. Steep, forested peaks and deep valleys diffused with rock formations characterize this state park that was settled in the early 1800s by simple farmers. But the land, so rich in coal and timber resources, was sold to the state for the establishment of the now infamous Brushy Mountain State Prison, and the resources were extracted using prison labor. The logging era ended in the 1920s and Frozen Head was declared a forest reserve. The Civilian Conservation Corps came in and established many of the trails that are in use today. A plaque at the main trailhead memorializes those who lost their lives developing the area. This is an ideal park for active people who like a small campground but want plenty of activities all within walking distance of the campground.

Frozen Head's campground is known as the Big Cove Camping Area. A figure-eight loop contains 20 sites that border Big Cove Branch and Flat Fork Creek. Big Cove backs up against Bird Mountain and has a minor slope. The sites have been leveled and are set up amid large boulders that came to rest untold eons ago from atop Bird Mountain. The strewn gray boulders give it the distinctive Cumberland Mountains feel. Second-growth hardwoods

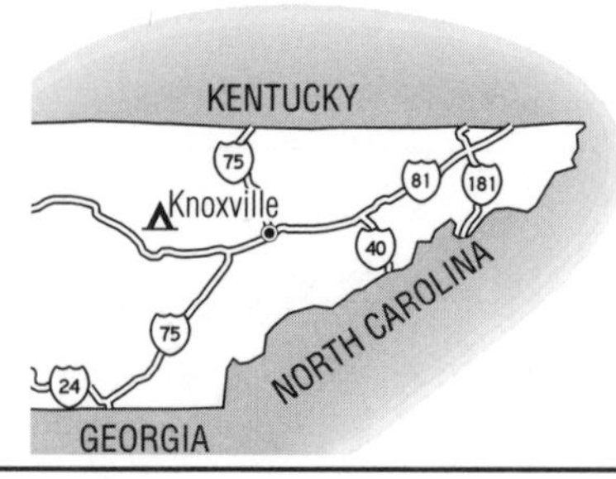

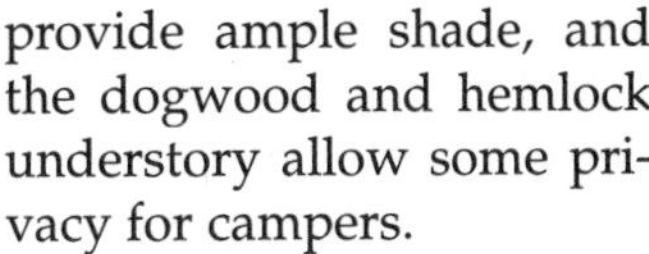

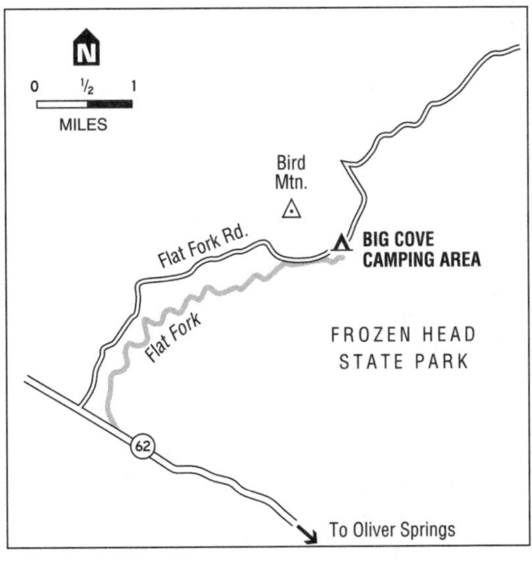

provide ample shade, and the dogwood and hemlock understory allow some privacy for campers.

A covered shed holds split firewood for campers to use. The new bathhouse sits close to all in the middle of the campground. Hot showers and flush toilets for each sex are kept in great condition. Two spigots provide drinking water for the small campground. Some sites are fairly close together, but all provide abundant room to spread out your gear. One group site is available for $17 per night. Ten sites allow tent and trailer camping; the other nine sites are for tents only. An overflow and off-season camping area is situated along Flat Fork Creek up from the regular campground. It has only a camping spot and a fire ring.

The park gates are closed from sunset to 8 A.M. Late-arriving campers must open and close the gate as they enter. It's best to get situated for the evening and stay within the park's confines. Actually, if you plan wisely, you won't even have to get back in your car until you leave for good; there's plenty to do. But if you forgot something, you can purchase supplies back in Oliver Springs, east on TN 62.

The trails of Frozen Head will take you to some fascinating places. The 3,324-foot Frozen Head Fire Tower is the apex of the trail system. You can see the surrounding highlands of the Cumberland Plateau and the Great Smoky Mountains in the distance. Other features include the Chimney Rock, a natural observation point that looks west as far as the eye can see. Or take the Spicewood Branch Trail .6 mile up to DeBord Falls. A mile farther is Emory

Gap Falls. The Lookout Tower and Bird Mountain trails leave directly from the campground.

Two miles farther on the Bird Mountain Trail is one of Frozen Head's defining rock formations, Castle Rock. This rock formation extends over 100 feet high and 300 feet wide; with a little imagination you can see the center edifice of the castle with turrets on both ends. These rock formations are the remnants of the erosion-resistant sandstone that covers the Cumberland Plateau. The softer rock and soil below this caprock eroded, leaving rock formations that seemingly jut straight out of the land. Bicyclers can stay on the Lookout Tower Trail and pedal all the way to the fire tower. Hikers can take this trail or many others to get their views from the tower.

If you don't feel like hiking or relaxing in the campground, there are many other activities. Play volleyball on one of the sand courts. Throw horseshoes at one of the three pits. Shoot some basketball at the outdoor court. There's even Ping-Pong. Check out the equipment you need free-of-charge at the park office. During the summer, many park activities take place at the 240-seat amphitheater, including interpretive talks, slide shows, movies, and music.

My trip intentionally coincided with spring's wildflower display. Frozen Head has one of the richest wildflower areas in the Southeast. I didn't even have to leave the campground to see purple, yellow, and white symbols of the season of rebirth. However, I did tramp many streamside trails and was glad this piece of the Cumberlands was preserved for all to enjoy.

KEY INFORMATION

Frozen Head State Park
964 Flat Fork Road
Wartburg, TN 37887

Operated by: Tennessee State Parks

Information: (423) 346-3318

Open: March 16 to October 31

Individual sites: 20

Each site has: Picnic table, fire grate/grill, lantern post, firewood

Site assignment: First come, first served

Registration: At Visitor Center

Facilities: Water, flush toilets, hot showers

Parking: At campsites only

Fee: $9.50 per night for 2 people; 50 cents each additional person

Elevation: 1,500 feet

Restrictions:

Pets—On leash at all times

Fires—In fire grates only

Alcoholic beverages—Prohibited

Vehicles—16-foot trailer limit due to narrow bridge crossing

Other—14-day stay limit

To get there, from Oak Ridge follow TN 62 west 4 miles to Oliver Springs. Drive 13 miles beyond Oliver Springs and turn right onto Flat Fork Road. A sign for Morgan County Regional Correctional Facility and Frozen Head State Park alert you to the right turn. Follow Flat Fork Road 4 miles to the entrance of Frozen Head State Park. The Visitor Center is on your right.

GEE CREEK CAMPGROUND

Etowah, Tennessee

CAMPGROUND RATINGS

Beauty:	★★★★★
Site privacy:	★★★★
Site spaciousness:	★★★★★
Quiet:	★★★
Security:	★★★★★
Cleanliness/upkeep:	★★★★★

It will take the Hiwassee River and Gee Creek Wilderness to tear you away from the tall pines of Gee Creek Campground.

Gee Creek Campground lies in a large, wooded flat at the base of Starr Mountain, adjacent to the cold, clear waters of the Hiwassee River. Hundreds of tall pines reach for the sky, providing an ideal amount of shade, yet allowing a cool breeze to drift through the campground. The sites are widely spaced along two loops that meander amid the pines. The clean campsites are placed well apart from each other for a maximum amount of spaciousness. Even without a lot of groundcover, the sheer number of trees and the distance between sites allow for adequate privacy. You never have to walk too far for water, as spigots are spread out along both loops. The campground is well maintained by state employees. A Tennessee State park ranger lives across from the campground for added security and emergency situations. The park office is south on U.S. 411 across the Hiwassee River.

Gee Creek is open all year, yet receives heavy use only on summer weekends. The bathhouse is located near the center of the campground and is open from mid-March to the end of November. In winter, port-a-toilets are used and showers are unavailable, though drinking water is still provided.

Our visit was during spring. Yellow pollen from the numerous pines dusted my Jeep and all our gear. Dogwoods bloomed above the needle-carpeted forest

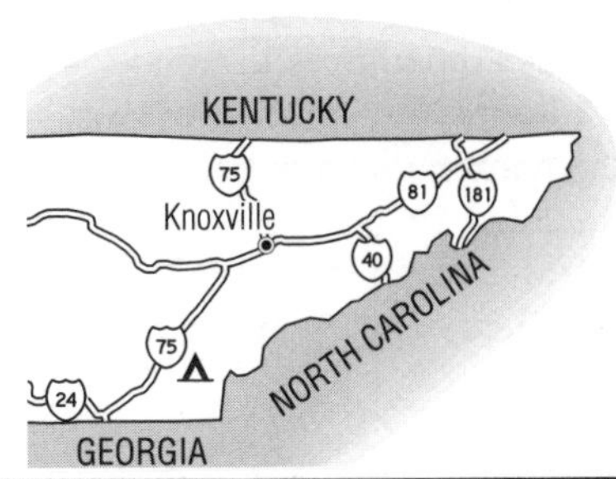

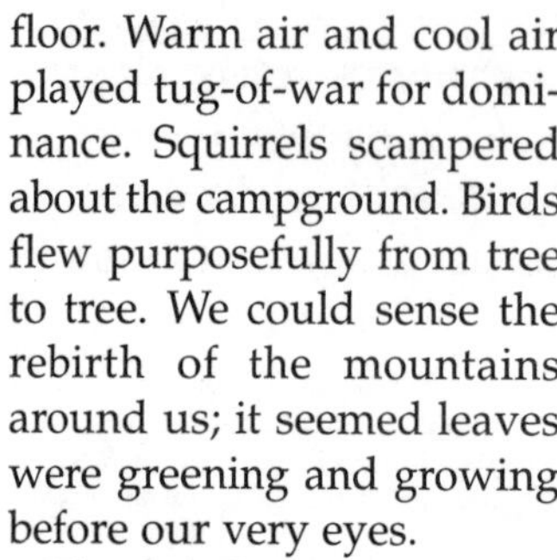

floor. Warm air and cool air played tug-of-war for dominance. Squirrels scampered about the campground. Birds flew purposefully from tree to tree. We could sense the rebirth of the mountains around us; it seemed leaves were greening and growing before our very eyes.

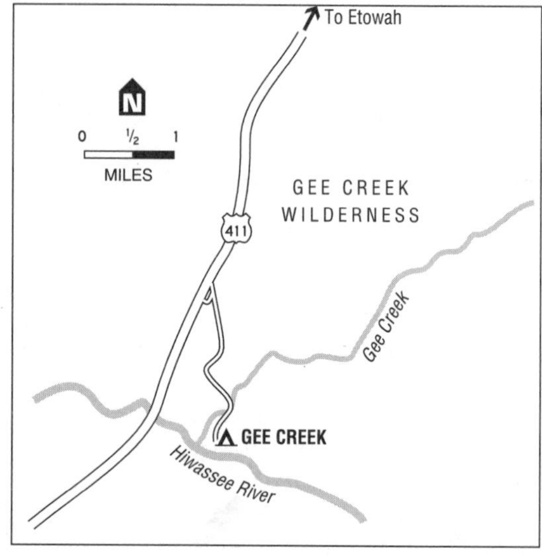

The Gee Creek Wilderness is only a short distance away and certainly worth a visit. Drive back to U.S. 411 and turn right. Then turn right at the sign for Gee Creek after half a mile. Follow the paved road over the railroad tracks, then turn right. Drive 2 miles until the road turns to gravel. The Gee Creek Watchable Wildlife Trail is on your left. Just a short distance beyond that is the Gee Creek Trail itself. Trace the old fisherman's trail up the gorge. Many small waterfalls provide plentiful photographic opportunities. The trail crosses the creek several times below old-growth hemlocks and dead-ends after 1.9 miles. On the return trip, look for the little things you missed on the way up. Rock climbers can climb some of the creekside bluffs, but be very careful.

The Gee Creek Watchable Wildlife Trail is a .7-mile trail designed to increase the hiker's knowledge of nature's signs. The Park Service has placed nest boxes, interpretive information, wildlife plantings, and a track pit to see which animals have passed this way. This is an excellent trail to get children interested in nature. Also starting at the Gee Creek trailhead is the Starr Mountain Trail (#190). It leads 4.8 miles up to the ridgeline of Starr Mountain and offers expansive views of the surrounding area.

After all this hiking, maybe you need to cool down. The Hiwassee River awaits and can be enjoyed in a number of ways. It drains over 750,000 acres of forested mountain land, resulting in clear and pure water. Informal trails lead to and along the river from the campground. Make sure young children are supervised. When the turbines upstream are generating, the water will be swift. Most water lovers enjoy the river by raft, canoe, funyak, or tube. No matter your watercraft, it's generally a 5.5-mile float through the splendid Cherokee National Forest. The water, primarily Class I and II on the international scale of difficulty, is very cold. The river is in the last stages of being designated a National Wild and Scenic River. Outfitters will supply anything you need, including a shuttle up the river if you have your own equipment. I recommend Hiwassee Outfitters. They are a reputable family operation. Call (800) 338-8133 for information.

The Hiwassee is also a mecca for trout fishermen. Anglers head to the river on foggy mornings to dance their flies before unsuspecting trout. If you want to try your luck and are ill-prepared, there are stores and outfitters who will get you on or in the water. The old train depot town of Etowah is 6 miles north on U.S. 411 if you need supplies.

To get there, from Etowah drive south on U.S. 411 for 6 miles. Turn left onto a signed, paved road for Gee Creek Campground and the Cherokee National Forest. Pass through an old field with houses. At one mile turn right into the Gee Creek Campground.

KEY INFORMATION

Gee Creek Campground
Hiwassee State Scenic River, Box 255
Delano, TN 37325

Operated by: Tennessee State Parks

Information: (423) 338-4133

Open: Year-round

Individual sites: 43

Each site has: Picnic table, grill, fire pit, lantern post

Site assignment: First come, first served; no reservations

Registration: Self-registration on site

Facilities: Drinking water, flush toilets, warm showers, soft-drink machines

Parking: At campsites only

Fee: $10 per night for 2 people, 50 cents each additional person

Elevation: 1,000 feet

Restrictions:

Pets—On leash only

Fires—In fire rings only

Alcoholic beverages—Prohibited

Vehicles—None

Other—14-day stay limit

HOLLY FLATS CAMPGROUND

Tellico Plains, Tennessee

If you place a high priority on barefoot tent camping, skip Holly Flats. The place is true to its name. Holly trees dot the cozy campground, shedding their prickly leaves to decay on the woodland floor. But if you don't mind wearing shoes while you camp, you'll love this place. It offers a variety of sites in a remote atmosphere with plenty to do nearby. The Bald River Gorge Wilderness is just across the gravel road, and Waucheesi Mountain and Warriors Passage National Recreation Trail are close as well.

Holly Flats has that old-time campground ambience: the smell of wood smoke and hamburgers cooking; sun filtering through the trees; cool mornings and lazy afternoons. This timeworn feel stems from the simple fact that the campground *is* old. The sites haven't been regraded in a long time, the picnic tables have their share of initials carved in them, and the fire rings are hand-placed, circular piles of rocks. But that's not all bad. The campground is like an old pair of favorite shoes: it may be worn and have a few scuff marks, but it sure is comfortable.

Cross the bridge over Bald River and the campground begins. Two sites are located in the grassy area by the bridge for sun lovers. Farther up, the campground splits into two roads that end in small loops. The first road splits off to the right away from Bald River. It has eight thickly wooded

CAMPGROUND RATINGS

Beauty:	★★★★
Site privacy:	★★★★
Site spaciousness:	★★★★★
Quiet:	★★★★★
Security:	★★★
Cleanliness/upkeep:	★★★

Shoes are a must in this old-time campground next door to the Bald River Wilderness.

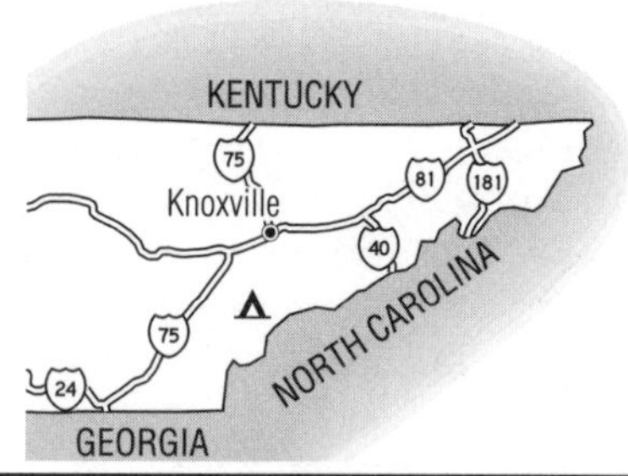

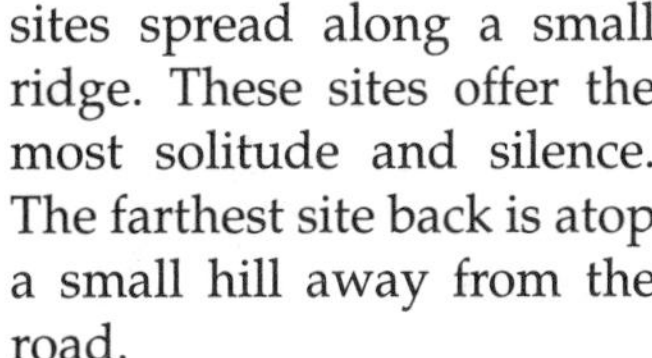

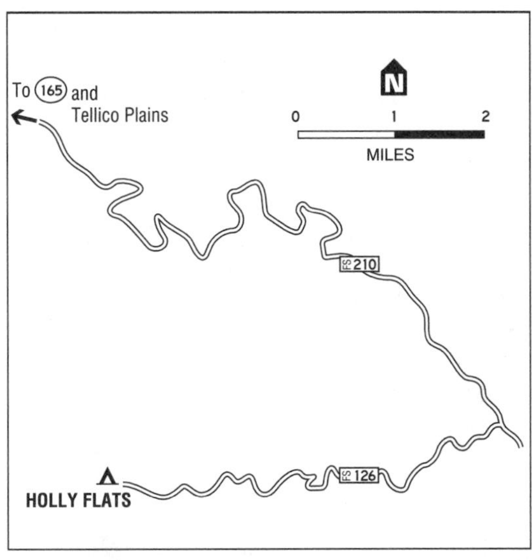

sites spread along a small ridge. These sites offer the most solitude and silence. The farthest site back is atop a small hill away from the road.

The second road runs next to Bald River. All six sites are directly riverside in a narrow flat. These campsites are more open, lying beneath large trees and covered with a holly and rhododendron understory. The melody of the river making its descent permeates the flat. A comfort station with vault toilets for each sex is on the side of the road opposite Bald River. Get your water from an old-fashioned hand pump where the two roads split apart. Holly Flats is a designated pack-it-in, pack-it-out campground. It has no trash receptacles. Pack out all your trash and any trash that thoughtless campers leave behind.

Several hiking trails start near Holly Flats. The Bald River Trail (#88) starts .4 mile west down the Bald River on Forest Service Road 126. It strikes through the heart of the 3,700-acre Bald River Gorge Wilderness. The trail leads 4.8 miles through the steep-sided gorge to Bald River Falls. It makes an excellent day hike. For those interested in angling, Bald River is a noted trout stream. The Kirkland Creek Trail (#85) starts .4 mile east of the campground on FS 126. A variety of forest types are represented along its route. The trail runs up a valley for 3 miles, then follows an old logging road to Sandy Gap and the North Carolina state line at 4.6 miles.

Less than one mile east of Holly Flats on FS 126 is the Brookshire Creek Trail (#180). It starts in an old field, crosses Bald River, and climbs 6 miles to the state line. Brookshire Creek has trout as well. Up the trail are some very remote old homesites where, in times past, subsistence mountain farmers battled the hills and the elements to carve out a living. A clearing lies at the end of the trail and makes a cool summertime picnic spot.

To get a sweat-free overlay of the land, drive to the top of 3,692-foot Waucheesi Mountain. Rangers used to watch for fires from an old tower there. Although it has since been torn down, views are still available from ground level. From Holly Flats drive west on FS 126 to FS 126C. Turn left and climb the mountain; FS 126C ends at the top. You can peer down into the Bald River Gorge and the Tellico River basin. The Warriors Passage National Recreation Trail (#164) starts partway up FS 126C on your right. The trail traces an old route used by the Cherokee on their travels between settlements and, later, by white traders and soldiers who eventually drove the Cherokee out. The historic trail leads one way for 5 miles to FS 76.

Holly Flats is a relaxing campground bordering one of Tennessee's finest wilderness areas. Give this slice of the Cherokee National Forest a try.

To get there, from Tellico Plains drive east on TN 165 for 5.3 miles. Turn right on FS 210. Follow it for 13.9 miles to FS 126. Turn right on gravel FS 126 and follow it for 6 miles. Holly Flats Campground will be across a bridge on your left.

KEY INFORMATION

Holly Flats Campground
250 Ranger Station Road
Tellico Plains, TN 37385

Operated by: U.S. Forest Service

Information: (423) 253-2520

Open: Year-round; access road subject to winter closure

Individual sites: 17

Each site has: Tent pad, picnic table, fire ring

Site assignment: First come, first served; no reservations

Registration: Self-registration on site

Facilities: Pumped water, vault toilet

Parking: At campsites only

Fee: $6 per night

Elevation: 2,150 feet

Restrictions:

Pets—On leash only

Fires—In fire rings only

Alcoholic beverages—At campsites only

Vehicles—None

Other—Pack it in; pack it out

JAKE BEST CAMPGROUND

Tellico Plains, Tennessee

Jake Best Campground lies in wooded solitude on a high bluff overlooking Citico Creek. The seven sites are spaciously arranged along a gravel loop road. The two most popular sites are creekside, below the bluff. Though the isolated encampment is in hilly terrain, the sites are level and well separated from one another. With so few sites, you'll never be bothered by the endless drone of other car campers coming and going along the loop road.

The campground and nearby stream are named for Jake Best, a settler from the mid-1800s, who had a house up the creek that bears his name. A clearing and some graves still mark the homesite. The camping area is fairly open by Southern Appalachian standards, but some trees were left to provide ample shade and privacy.

The allure of Jake Best is its primitive setting. You're one with nature here. In fact, a bear country notice is posted at the fee area, so do not let too much distance get between you and your food. The pump well has been disconnected. Get your water from the creek, but treat or boil all water before consuming it. During my Jake Best experience, I got up one morning and stumbled down to the creek to get water for coffee. In my sleepy state I actually stumbled *into* the creek, soaking my lower half. That did a better job of waking me up than the coffee would have!

CAMPGROUND RATINGS

Beauty:	★★★★★
Site privacy:	★★★★
Site spaciousness:	★★★★
Quiet:	★★★★★
Security:	★★★★
Cleanliness/upkeep:	★★★★

Jake Best Campground makes a peaceful headquarters for exploring nearby Citico Creek Wilderness.

This rustic campground is only 10 linear miles from the Great Smoky Mountains National Park and offers scenery and history that rival that of the national park itself. In years past, this was Cherokee country. Indian names for area landmarks are spread throughout the land. The name Citico is derived from the Cherokee word *sitiku,* which means "clean fishing waters." They still are. The clear water of Citico Creek has quite a nip to it, even in summer.

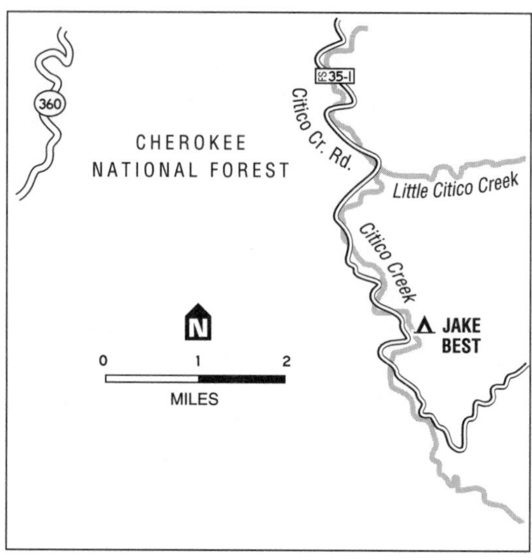

After the Cherokee came the lumberjack. The logging era lasted into the 1920s. A railroad ran along Citico Creek and its tributaries; its remains can still be seen today. The logging harvest devastated the land through a series of clearcuts, stream siltings, and wildfires. When the logging stopped, settlers moved in. Next, the Forest Service bought the land. A Civilian Conservation Corps camp was converted into the campground we see today. The surrounding watershed continues to return to its former natural character—so much so that in 1984 the upper section of the Citico Creek watershed was recognized for its exceptional beauty and was designated a wilderness.

Jake Best Campground is an ideal base camp for exploring the Citico Wilderness. A series of trails leave from Doublecamp Road (Forest Service Road 59). From Jake Best, drive 4 miles up Citico Creek Road (FS 35-1). Turn left to reach FS 59. I have hiked and camped throughout this wilderness and strongly recommend the following hikes. The Crowder Branch Trail (#84) starts 3.5 miles up FS 59. It leads 2.6 miles along a charming mountain stream through impressive woods to end at Crowder Place. An old homesite, Crowder Place has a reliable spring and an open meadow for your picnicking pleasure. At 6.7 miles on FS 59 you'll find Farr Gap and the Fodderstack Trail. The path leads along Fodderstack Ridge, allowing intermittent views of the surrounding wilderness and the Smokies beyond.

Drive 5.6 miles up Citico Creek Road (FS 35-1), then left for a short distance on FS 26 to the jumping off point for numerous trailheads that lead into the wilderness. Take the South Fork Citico Trail (#105) and delve deep into the mountains. The old, square building with no roof was once the camp commissary and powder magazine for the logging camp known as Jeffrey. Other history, both human and natural, awaits you down the trail.

On our trip here, during a late-winter weekend, we had the campground to ourselves. We chose a sunny site, enjoying those first warm rays that signal the impending arrival of spring. That night, a full moon rose over Cowcamp Ridge and shone so brightly we cooked our supper over the fire without any artificial light.

If you need supplies, go to Citico Beach Store. It is located in an old house 8 miles down FS 35-1. It's every bit as countrified as the whole area. But try to bring in all your supplies, as Jake Best is pretty far from the civilized world. And that can be good. You will enjoy this land that probably would have been a national park itself had the unmatched Smokies not been so close.

KEY INFORMATION

Jake Best Campground
250 Ranger Station Road
Tellico Plains, TN 37385

Operated by: U.S. Forest Service

Information: (423) 253-2520

Open: Year-round

Individual sites: 7

Each site has: Graveled tent pad, picnic table, rock fire ring, lantern post

Site assignment: First come, first served; no reservations

Registration: Self-registration on site

Facilities: Pit toilet

Parking: At individual sites

Fee: $6 per night

Elevation: 1,300 feet

Restrictions:

Pets—Confined to leash or under physical control at all times

Fires—In fire rings only

Alcoholic beverages—At campsites only

Vehicles—At campsites only

Other—14-day stay limit

To get there, from the town square in Tellico Plains, drive south on TN 165 for .5 mile. Turn left on TN 360 and drive 9 miles to Monroe County 504, also known as Buck Highway. A sign to Citico Creek will mark your right turn. After the right turn, drive 5.1 miles to FS 35-1. Make sure to veer left at the junction with Monroe County 506. After turning right on FS 35-1, drive 2.9 miles to Jake Best Campground on your left.

TENNESSEE

LITTLE OAK CAMPGROUND

Bristol, Tennessee

Lakeside camping is a breeze at Little Oak. It is sizable and well laid out, lying atop the remnants of Little Oak Mountain after the Holston River Valley was flooded to create South Holston Lake. Though large, Little Oak is widely dispersed on four loops that jut into the lake. This arrangement allows for many spacious lakeside sites, and each loop feels like its own little campground. Short paths slope from each lakeside site to the water's edge. There are so many attractive sites from which to choose. This campground was designed for a pleasant camping experience, not just a way station for the urban masses to cram into. We drove each loop so many times, seeing one ideal site and then seeing an even better one; we were sure another camper was going to turn in our license plate to a ranger.

Just beyond the pay station is the Hemlock Loop. It contains 14 sites nestled beneath a thick stand of hemlock trees. Most of the sites are on the outside of the loop, well away from one another with plenty of cover between sites. An old-fashioned vault toilet and a modern comfort station with flush toilets and showers are at the head of the loop. Camp at Hemlock Loop if you like very shady sites.

Lone Pine Loop is for those who prefer sunny sites. Two small fields lie adjacent to the loop and allow more light into the camping areas. Three comfort stations are

CAMPGROUND RATINGS

Beauty:	★★★★
Site privacy:	★★★★
Site spaciousness:	★★★★★
Quiet:	★★★
Security:	★★★★★
Cleanliness/upkeep:	★★★★

Picking the best campsite will be your biggest problem at Little Oak. Both aquatic and earthly endeavors await your arrival.

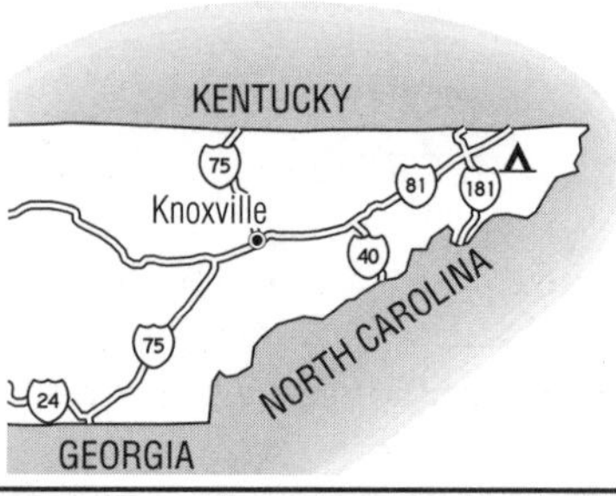

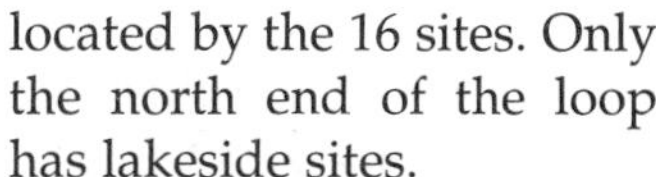

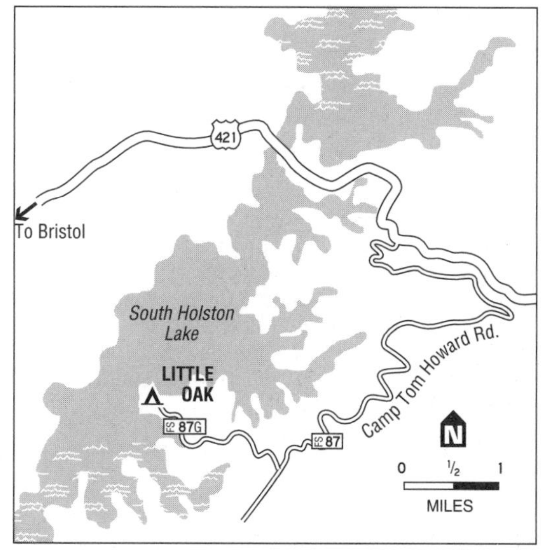

located by the 16 sites. Only the north end of the loop has lakeside sites.

Big Oak Loop has 16 sites and is located on a spit of hardwoods and evergreens that juts north into the lake. Nearly all the sites are lakeside. A modern comfort station is located halfway along the loop, and water faucets are nearby. The view from Big Oak Loop into South Holston Lake is my personal favorite.

Poplar Loop is the largest loop with 23 sites, but the sites are split into two loops of their own, facing west and south into the lake. A modern comfort station is at each loop. Most of these sites are lakeside.

We finally settled on Big Oak Loop. After setting up camp, we watched the sun turn into a red ball of fire over South Holston Lake. Gentle waves lapped at our feet as we sat along the shoreline. We took a vigorous hike in the cool of the next morning on the Little Oak Trail that loops the outer peninsula of the campground. This campground is virtually surrounded by the lake, giving it a very aquatic ambience. For a different perspective, take the Little Oak Mountain Trail. It leaves the campground near the pay station and circles back after a jaunt into the woods. For yet another perspective on Little Oak, get out on the lake itself. A boat ramp is conveniently situated between the Hemlock and Poplar loops. Swim, fish, or take a pleasure ride up the lake into the state of Virginia.

In East Tennessee, the high country is never far away. Little Oak is near the Flint Mill Scenic Area, which has a broad representation of Southern Appalachian flora and fauna and elevations exceeding 4,000 feet. Turn right out of the campground onto Forest Service Road 87 and drive a short 1.4 miles. The Josiah Trail (Forest Trail #50) starts on your left and ascends for 2.2 miles to a saddle on Holston Mountain and Forest Trail #44. To your left at 4.3 miles is the Appalachian Trail and the Double Springs Gap backcountry shelter. To your right after 3.4 miles is the Holston Mountain Fire Tower and views aplenty. Flint Mill Trail (FT #49) climbs 1 steep mile to Flint Rock and some fantastic views of South Holston Lake. The trail is 2.2 miles on the left past the Josiah Trail.

A public pay telephone is located at the pay station. Fishing equipment and all supplies are available back in Bristol.

To get there, from Bristol take U.S. 421 east for 14 miles. Turn right on Camp Tom Howard Road (FS 87) at signed intersection for Little Oak Campground. Follow FS 87 for 6.5 miles. Turn right on FS 87G. Follow it for 1.5 miles and dead end into Little Oak Recreation Area.

KEY INFORMATION

Little Oak Campground
Route 9, Box 2235
Elizabethton, TN 37643

Operated by: U.S. Forest Service

Information: (423) 542-2942

Open: April 21 to November 31

Individual sites: 72

Each site has: Tent pad, picnic table, fire grate, lantern post

Site assignment: First come, first served; no reservations

Registration: Self-registration on site

Facilities: Water faucets, flush toilets, warm showers

Parking: At campsites only

Fee: $10 per night

Elevation: 1,750 feet

Restrictions:

Pets—On leash only

Fires—In fire grates only

Alcoholic beverages—Prohibited

Vehicles—None

Other—14-day stay limit

NORTH RIVER CAMPGROUND

Tellico Plains, Tennessee

North River Campground is located deep within the Cherokee National Forest. A serene atmosphere pervades the campground. It is situated on a level river bend between a wooded mountainside and the clear-running North River. For a tent camper who likes a minimum of fanfare and a maximum of nature, this is the place.

Human accoutrements are sparse in this Forest Service campground, but natural amenities are abundant. Trout ply the waters of the creek, shaded by hemlock, sycamore, and rhododendron. Mature dogwoods and white pine provide a beautiful backdrop for those relaxing evenings fireside. Grassy areas grow between the trees, accentuating the ample spaciousness between the level tent sites. Dead, fallen firewood is abundant in the area, as are nature's citizens: deer, wild turkey, wild boar, and bear.

With only 11 sites in the entire campground, quiet is the rule here. The North River will lull you to sleep at night and the birds will be your alarm clock in the morning. For the water lover, 8 of the 11 sites are actually riverside. Two of the sites could qualify as group sites, with double picnic tables, additional tent pads, and ample parking for family camping. For contrast, the lower end of the campground is more shaded and isolated, while the upper end is more open and sunny.

CAMPGROUND RATINGS

Beauty:	★★★★★
Site privacy:	★★★★★
Site spaciousness:	★★★★★
Quiet:	★★★★★
Security:	★★★★
Cleanliness/upkeep:	★★★★

Let this slice of riverine Southern Appalachia be your quiet woodland escape.

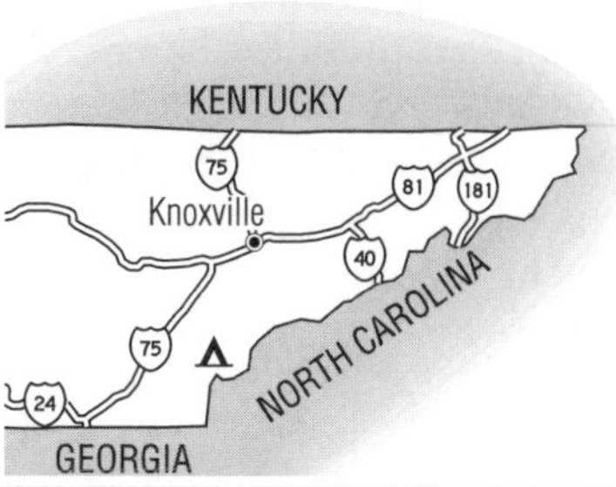

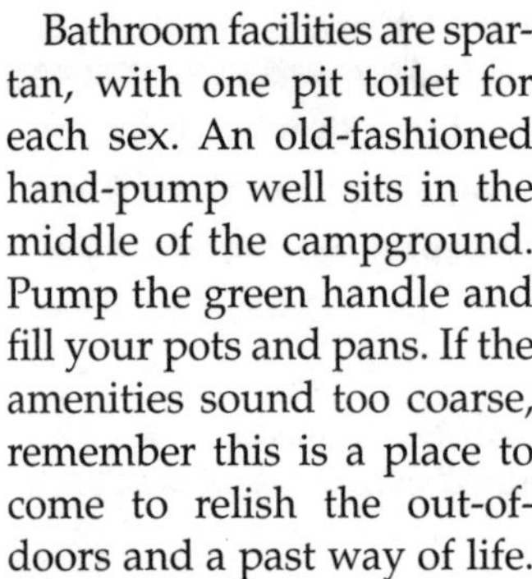

Bathroom facilities are spartan, with one pit toilet for each sex. An old-fashioned hand-pump well sits in the middle of the campground. Pump the green handle and fill your pots and pans. If the amenities sound too coarse, remember this is a place to come to relish the out-of-doors and a past way of life.

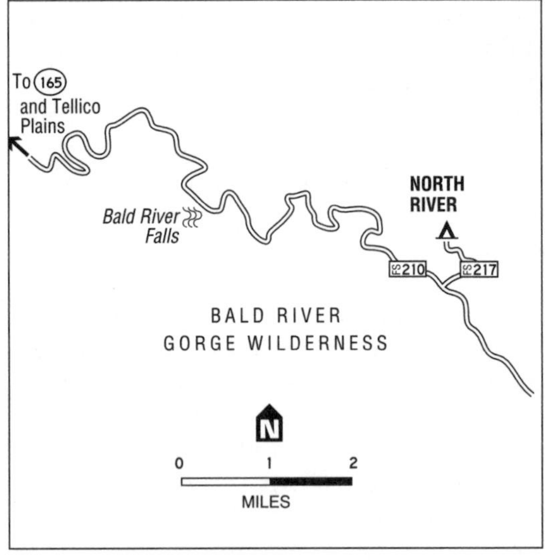

Beard cane, a species of the grass family, grows along the North River at the campground. The leaves on the main stem of the cane form the "beard" of this plant, once used as a fishing pole by old-time mountaineers. Modern day anglers prefer to fly fish and are inspired by a trip to the nearby Pheasant Fields Fish Hatchery, 4.5 miles away. Turn right out of the campground and turn right again at .1 mile on Forest Service Road 216. Go 1 mile and turn left up FS 210 for 3.5 miles. Whether you fish or not, check it out. Rainbow trout are raised at the hatchery for stocking, and in one of the many tanks there are some lunkers that will cause your eyes to bulge in disbelief.

If you get the urge to explore, stretch your legs on the Sycamore Creek Trail (Forest Trail #61), which starts at the fish hatchery. Sycamore Creek is the feeder stream for the hatchery. The trail leads up to Whigg Meadow, an open field nearly a mile high, sporting views into Citico Creek/Slickrock Wilderness. Nearby, down FS 217 from the campground, are the McNabb and Hemlock Creek trails (#92 and #101, respectively). These trails are located in the Brushy Ridge Primitive Area just across from the campground. Each footpath follows a scenic tributary of the North River up to the high country. Before darkness falls, grab your camera and drive back to Bald River Falls for some scenic shots of this panoramic waterfall.

While exploring the area, my friends and I came to a rough road a few miles beyond the hatchery, just over the North Carolina line. We followed it for a distance because I wanted to show them where I had become stuck fording the Tellico River. As we came upon the crossing, we found a frustrated couple standing by their four-wheel-drive vehicle. It was stuck in the very place that mine had been stuck a decade earlier! We pulled them out with a chain and turned around, laughing at the irony of the situation.

You can purchase supplies during summer months in the small community of Green Cove. It is a private inholding in the national forest, consisting of summer cottages, a little motel, a small country store, and a gas station. Green Cove is located two miles from the campground up FS 210 before the fish hatchery.

If you want to camp in a national forest surrounded by natural beauty, come to the North River Campground. It is literally encircled by mountainous woodland and is spacious enough that you never feel packed in. Fellow campers are likely to be friendly locals of Monroe County who generally will help you in any way they can.

To get there, from the town square in Tellico Plains, drive 4.7 miles south on TN 165 to FS 210. Turn right on FS 210 and drive 9.6 miles to FS 217, passing Tellico Ranger Station at .4 mile, where you might want to obtain a forest map. Also pass Bald River Falls at 6.3 miles. Turn left 3.3 miles past the falls on FS 217. Follow FS 217 for 3 miles. North River Campground will be on your right.

KEY INFORMATION

North River Campground
250 Ranger Station Road
Tellico Plains, TN 37385

Operated by: U.S. Forest Service

Information: (423) 253-2520

Open: Year-round

Individual sites: 11

Each site has: Graveled tent pad, picnic table, fire ring, lantern holder

Site assignment: First come, first served; no reservations

Registration: Self-registration on site

Facilities: Pump-well water, pit toilet

Parking: At individual sites

Fee: $6 per night

Elevation: 1,840 feet

Restrictions:

Pets—Confined to leash or under physical control at all times

Fires—In fire rings only

Alcoholic beverages—At campsites only

Vehicles—At campsites only

Other—14-day stay limit

PAINT CREEK CAMPGROUND

Greeneville, Tennessee

The windshield wipers squeaked a decidedly unenthusiastic mantra the day we set out for Paint Creek. As we wound down the saturated gravel road, the camping trip seemed more like a job than an outing. But our prospects brightened beyond the small bridge spanning Paint Creek. To our left lay the welcome sight of the Paint Creek Campground.

Well laid out on an inside bend of Paint Creek, this cozy campground blends with its surroundings so well that you'll think it was meant for tent camping all along. Each campsite is ideally situated among the trees of the forest and outlined with wood timbers that hold freshly spread gravel, offering an attractive and well-drained site. Eleven of the sites are directly creekside, but there are no bad sites at this campground. They're all large and well distanced from one another by thick stands of eastern hemlock, with plenty of room to pitch a tent and spread out a carload of gear.

Two small loops, each with one group site, divide the campground. Vault toilets for each sex are unobtrusively placed on each loop. An old-fashioned hand-pump well is located at the campground entrance. The north loop has only six sites; half are along Paint Creek, a stream any mountain would be proud to bear. The other 15 sites are on the south loop, which follows Paint

CAMPGROUND RATINGS

Beauty:	★★★★★
Site privacy:	★★★★★
Site spaciousness:	★★★★★
Quiet:	★★★★
Security:	★★★★
Cleanliness/upkeep:	★★★★

Backed against the Bald Mountains, Paint Creek is situated for exploring the beautiful Greene County highlands and historic Greeneville, home of Andrew Johnson.

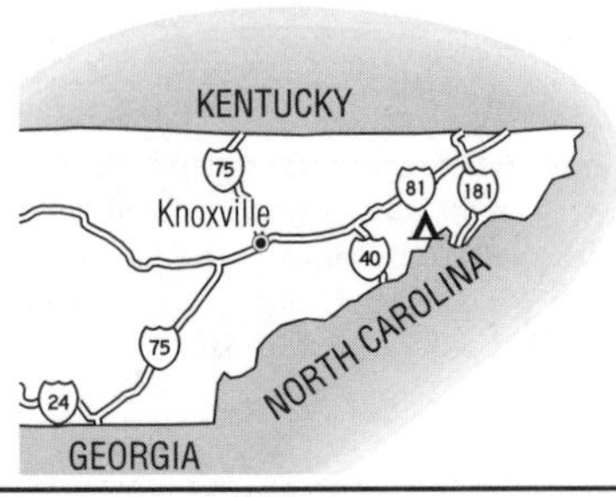

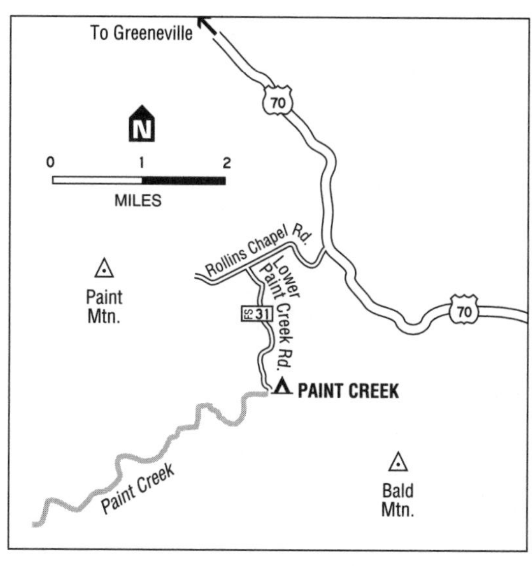

Creek as it descends toward the French Broad River.

The early spring sky cleared as we set up camp; the place was our own. After lunch we went for a drive along Forest Service Road 41 paralleling Paint Creek to see Dudley Falls, which spills into a big pool backed by a rocky bluff. It's a popular swimming hole during warm weather months. The road bridged the creek and made its way near smaller falls and fishing holes, meandering a few miles to Paint Creek's confluence with the French Broad River at Paint Rock. We scanned the French Broad, cut deep into the mountains. Directly across the river lay Huff Island, its banks nearly scoured from high water. The French Broad is a popular canoeing and rafting river. Outfitters are stationed in Del Rio, Tennessee, or across the mountain in Hot Springs, North Carolina.

The Appalachian Trail is very accessible from Paint Creek. Turn left out of the campground and up FS 31 for 5 miles to Hurricane Gap. The AT passes through the gap. Follow the AT to your right for .8 mile up to the Rich Mountain Fire Tower, at an elevation of 3,643 feet. Look down on the French Broad Valley and gaze at the Bald Mountains around you. Mount Mitchell, the highest point east of the Mississippi River at 6,682 feet, is to the east.

On our way back home we stopped in Greeneville, established in 1781. A well-preserved town of old, brick buildings, this town's citizens have placed a special emphasis on keeping up the many historic sites in the area. It is the site of Civil War skirmishes and home of President Andrew Johnson. His time in office was troubled, starting with the assumption of the presidency after the assassination of Abraham Lincoln and ending with near impeachment by the Senate during Reconstruction. The native sons of Greeneville are proud of their president. The National Park Service maintains a Visitor Center in town. Greeneville's historic downtown has undergone a revitalization and restoration of its historic structures. Park your car and check out Johnson's home and tailor shop, in addition to old churches, the Stone Jail, and the Harmony Cemetery.

To get there, from Greeneville take U.S. 70 south for 12.5 miles. Turn right on Rollins Chapel Road. Drive 1.1 miles. Then turn left on Lower Paint Creek Road. The pavement ends after 1.1 miles. Continue downhill for another .5 mile and cross Paint Creek on a small bridge. The Paint Creek Campground is on your left.

KEY INFORMATION

Paint Creek Campground
124 Austin Street, Suite #3
Greeneville, TN 37743

Operated by: U.S. Forest Service

Information: (423) 638-4109

Open: April 15 to December 15

Individual sites: 21

Each site has: Fire grate, picnic table, lantern post, tent pad

Site assignment: First come, first served; no reservations

Registration: Self-registration on site

Facilities: Pump water, vault toilets

Parking: At campsites only

Fee: $6 per night; $10 per night for group sites

Elevation: 1,640 feet

Restrictions:

Pets—On a 6-foot leash only

Fires—In fire grates only

Alcoholic beverages—At campsites only

Vehicles—Trailers up to 26 feet

Other—14-day stay limit

PICKETT STATE PARK

Jamestown, Tennessee

CAMPGROUND RATINGS

Beauty: ★★★★
Site privacy: ★★★
Site spaciousness: ★★★
Quiet: ★★★★
Security: ★★★★★
Cleanliness/upkeep: ★★★★

Tennessee's first state park is 11,750 acres of scenic botanical and geologic wonders.

Tennessee State Parks come fully loaded with man-made amenities to make the most of your visit. But Pickett State Park was already fully loaded with natural features long before it became Tennessee's first state park way back in the 1930s. The campground is vintage, too. It is evident that over the years, Pickett's natural beauty, as well as the campground, have passed through caring hands.

The campground is situated atop a wooded hill. It has the standard circular loop configuration with a road bisecting the center of the loop, making almost a figure eight. You'll climb as you enter the loop. Most sites are on the outer edge of the loop, but the road that bisects the loop also has campsites along it. Tall pines and hardwoods shade the camping area. A light understory is prevalent, mixed with more heavily wooded sections, especially outside the main loop.

The campground was built before RVs existed, so, even though 31 of 40 sites have both water and electricity, it is primarily a tenter's campground. Water is nearby for the other nine sites. A modern bathhouse with flush toilets and hot showers and a coin laundry are in the very center of the campground. Those staying on the campground's perimeter may have to walk a bit to reach the bathhouse.

Hand-laid stone walls complement the natural surroundings. The campground

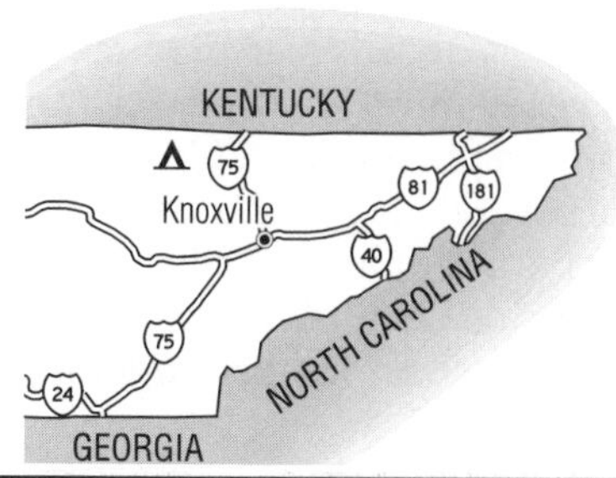

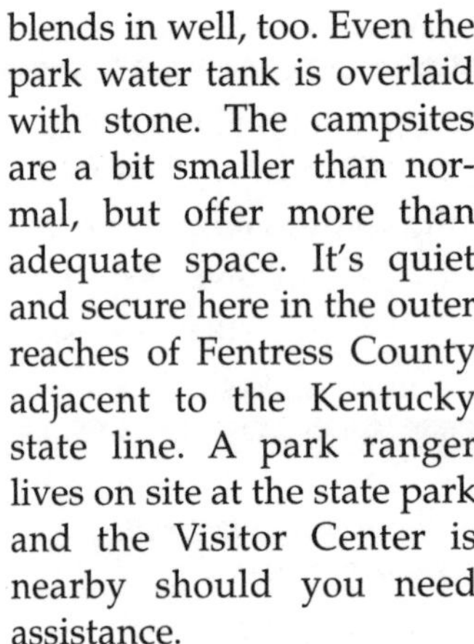

blends in well, too. Even the park water tank is overlaid with stone. The campsites are a bit smaller than normal, but offer more than adequate space. It's quiet and secure here in the outer reaches of Fentress County adjacent to the Kentucky state line. A park ranger lives on site at the state park and the Visitor Center is nearby should you need assistance.

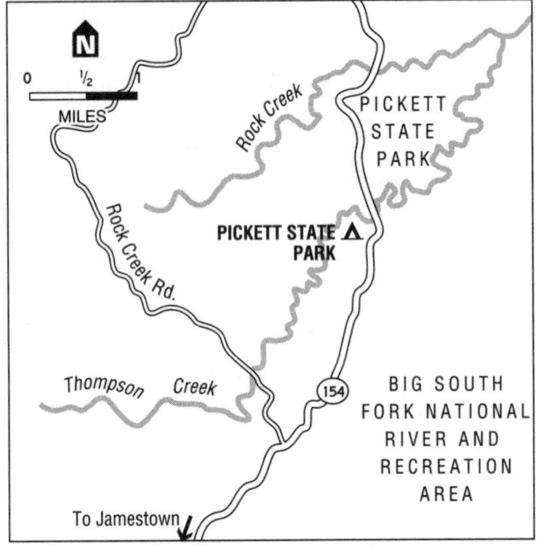

You may need help figuring out just what to do. Man-made pursuits include tennis, archery, badminton, horseshoes, and volleyball. Any equipment you may need is available free of charge at the park office. Before you visualize a wooded health club, there's a lot more as you make the transition from man-made to all-natural fun.

A swimming beach is open during the summer months at Arch Lake. This 15-acre, S-shaped lake offers trout fishing and canoe and rowboat rentals. A park naturalist is on duty during the summer. Headquarters are at the nature center, which is in the middle of the campground. Campfire programs and movies are also part of Pickett activities.

Finally, there are the landforms, without which no man-made state park could've been created. Much of the state forest escaped the logger's ax. Today, over 58 miles of trails trace beneath the trees, reaching natural bridges, caves, waterfalls, and rock bluffs.

Several short trails serve to loosen your legs. The Indian Rockhouse Trail travels .2 mile to a huge rock overhang with a water feature in its center. The 2.5-mile Lake Trail Loop crosses Arch Lake on a swinging bridge, then passes a natural bridge before looping back to the picnic area. It is 1 mile down to Double Falls from Thompson Overlook. The Hazard Cave Loop extends for 2.5 miles and goes by a sand-floored cave, then by the Natural Bridge, over 80 feet long and 20 feet high.

The two primary park trails are Rock Creek and Hidden Passage. The Rock Creek Trail parallels its namesake, passing small waterfalls in a classic, deeply wooded mountain stream. It is 5 miles one way and connects to the Sheltowee Trace Trail. The Sheltowee Trace Trail extends 250 miles into Kentucky. *Sheltowee* is Indian for "Big Turtle," which is what the local Indians called Daniel Boone way back when he was adopted into the Shawnee Tribe.

The master trail of Pickett is the 10-mile Hidden Passage Trail. The first feature you'll see is a modest arch, then comes the Hidden Passage, a small passageway created by a large rock overhang amid jumbled rocks. Next is Crystal Falls. On down you'll see overlooks and numerous rock houses, some with chestnut benches built during the Civilian Conservation Corps days. Take the Hidden Passage challenge. It will be a day you'll remember.

A rough trail map is available at the Visitor Center. They'll be glad to help you find a trail to suit your desires. This is one place where you can stay busy for days with all types of activities. Just make sure to get all your food and supplies back in Jamestown. You'll need the calories.

To get there, from Jamestown take U.S. 127 north for 2 miles to TN 154. Turn right on TN 154 and follow it for 10 miles. The park entrance will be on your left.

KEY INFORMATION

Pickett State Park
Polk Creek Route, Box 174
Jamestown, TN 38556

Operated by: Tennessee State Parks

Information: (615) 879-5821

Open: Year-round

Individual sites: 40

Each site has: Tent pad, fire grate, lantern post, picnic table

Site assignment: First come, first served; no reservations

Registration: At Visitor Center

Facilities: Piped water, flush toilets, showers, laundry, electrical hookups

Parking: At campsites only

Fee: $9.50 per night for 2 people; 50 cents each additional person

Elevation: 1,500 feet

Restrictions:

Pets—On a leash only

Fires—In fire grates only

Alcoholic beverages—Prohibited

Vehicles—None

Other—14-day stay limit

ROAN MOUNTAIN STATE PARK

Elizabethton, Tennessee

CAMPGROUND RATINGS

Beauty: ★★★★
Site privacy: ★★★★
Site spaciousness: ★★★★
Quiet: ★★★
Security: ★★★★★
Cleanliness/upkeep: ★★★★★

Roan Mountain State Park Campground is suitable, but the nearby highlands of Roan will make your stay extraordinary.

Combine the natural beauty of the heights of Roan with a first-class state park and you have the Roan Mountain experience, a worthwhile endeavor for any tent camper. Roan Mountain State Park Campground is attractive and well kept. The tent-camping-only area makes this campground practicable. Many activities can be undertaken without leaving your site. And it's only a 10-mile drive from the campground to the top of Roan Mountain and the Appalachian crest. The views near and far are breathtaking, meaning it may take a little longer to come down from this "high."

First, set up camp. Roan Mountain State Park Campground is divided into two distinct sections. Across the Doe River are 50 sites on a slope with three bathhouses and numerous water spigots. There are too many RVs here, but take a site if you must. The second camping area has 37 more RV and tent sites on one loop that you must drive through to get to the second loop. Before you become downcast, the second loop has 20 tent-only sites! And they will do the trick.

The tent-only loop is just east of the Doe River. The lush camping area is heavily wooded, with a thick canopy overhead. Rhododendron thickets mesh together between the sites, making for very private camping. Six sites are on the inside of the

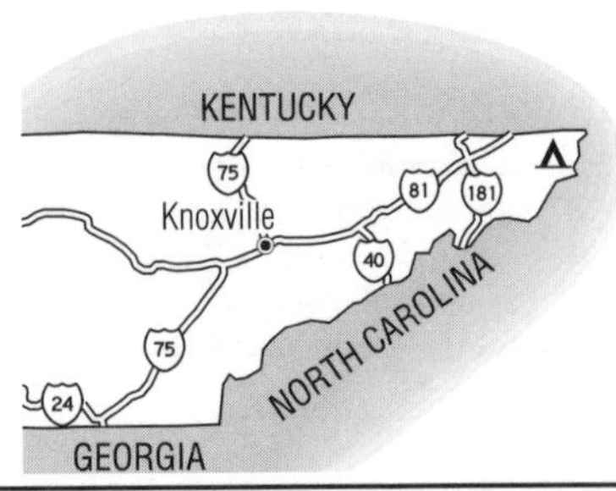

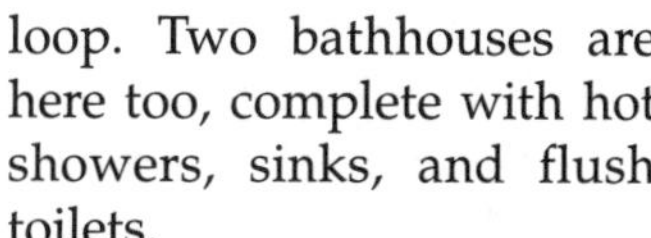

loop. Two bathhouses are here too, complete with hot showers, sinks, and flush toilets.

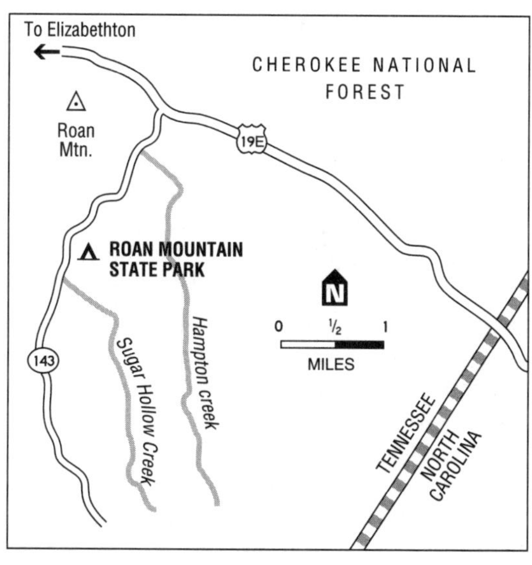

The other 14 sites are on the outside of the loop. Five special sites lie along the Doe River. Planners designed all the sites in the tent-only area with more than adequate room to spread your gear around. However, the sheer number of campers in the whole campground may make it a bit noisy at times. Fear not, this is a family-style campground, virtually devoid of "rough" people. A campground host and ranger-in-residence should further allay any safety concerns.

A short foot trail leads from the tenters' loop to the park pool, tennis courts, and playground. Badminton, volleyball, and other equipment can be checked out free of charge at the park office. Should you and your crew opt for the near and natural, two hiking trails take off from the campground itself. The Behrand Trail switchbacks into Bearwallow Hollow before heading north down to the Doe River and looping into the campground after 2.5 miles. Or take the short jaunt on the half-mile Tom Gray Trail.

The Raven Rock Overlook Trail starts just across from the campground pavilion and climbs to a scenic viewing area. Loop back on the Forest Road Trail for a 3-mile trek. You can also connect into the Cabin Loop Trail from the pavilion.

Two short trails embark from the Visitor Center, which itself contains an interesting historical artifact display. The .4-mile Peg Leg Mine Trail will take you back in time to the old mining days. Learn about the natural world of the park on the 1-mile Cloudland High Nature Trail Loop. From here you can hook into the Chestnut Ridge Trail and visit the Dave Miller historic homestead. It is an authentic pioneer farm that hearkens back to mountain life a century ago. You can also drive to the homestead.

After that tune-up, the best is yet to come. Get in your auto and turn right out of the campground. Make the winding drive into the high country and the state line at Carvers Gap (elevation 5,512 feet). The Appalachian Trail passes through here. To the left is a series of open meadows, called "balds," that are unmatched anywhere in the Appalachian Range. It is a .4-mile hike along the Appalachian Trail to the top of the first bald, named Round Bald. Beyond Round Bald, you can see—if it isn't foggy, which it often is—that the balds extend for miles, offering panoramic views unmatched anywhere in the Southeast.

Turn right just beyond Carvers Gap on Cloudland Road to the gardens of Roan Mountain and the mountain summit at 6,285 feet. The expanse of Catawba rhododendron covers over 600 acres, the largest natural rhododendron garden in the world. In June, the pinkish-purple flowers bloom in all their glory. It is but one of over 300 plant species that grow up here. Mountain winds here *average* 25 miles per hour year-round. In the winter, cross-country skiers take in the snowy scenery. Roan Mountain is a fantastic sight to behold any time of the year.

To get there, from Elizabethton take U.S. 19E east for 16 miles to TN 143. Turn right on TN 143 and follow it for 3 miles to Roan Mountain State Park.

KEY INFORMATION

Roan Mountain State Park
Route 1, Box 236
Roan Mountain, TN 37687

Operated by: Tennessee State Parks

Information: (423) 772-3303

Open: May 15 to October 31

Individual sites: 20 tent only; plus 87 RV and tent

Each site has: Tent pad, picnic table, fire grate, lantern post

Site assignment: 40% sites reserved; 60% first come, first served

Registration: (800) 250-8620 or at campground office

Facilities: Hot showers, flush toilets, pump water, laundry, pay phones

Parking: At campsites only

Fee: $9.50 per night for 1 or 2 people; 50 cents for each additional person per night

Elevation: 3,000 feet

Restrictions:

Pets—On leash only

Fires—In fire grates only

Alcoholic beverages—Prohibited

Vehicles—None

Other—Only one household family per site

ROCK CREEK CAMPGROUND

Erwin, Tennessee

Rock Creek Campground is a positive outcome of the Great Depression. Back in the 1930s, the Civilian Conservation Corps developed the area for forest recreation. As an antidote for an ailing economy, the Corps was assembled to provide jobs for unemployed men. Detractors of the organization accused the CCC of doing "make-work." Here at Rock Creek, the Corps introduced the works of man into the wilds of East Tennessee to provide further enjoyment of the Cherokee National Forest. What a fine area they had to start with! The national forest is fraught with virgin timberland and clear mountain streams that nestle against the backbone of the Unaka Mountains. Of course, the Forest Service has improved and maintained the area since the days of the Corps. But the old-time feel remains, as well as most of the original infrastructure. Today, as then, we can camp in the cool, shady cove of Rock Creek.

The campground is arranged in three loops. Mother Nature landscaped this place well, with tall hardwoods looming over a thick understory of moss, ferns, rhododendron, and small trees amid gray boulders. Rock Creek Campground has a deep-woods feel. The farther back you go in the cove, the more rustic the roomy campground becomes. The white noise of Rock Creek is your constant companion here.

CAMPGROUND RATINGS

Beauty:	★★★★★
Site privacy:	★★★★
Site spaciousness:	★★★★
Quiet:	★★★★
Security:	★★★★★
Cleanliness/upkeep:	★★★★

Camp in the cool and shady Rock Creek Campground adjacent to the impressive Unaka Mountain Wilderness.

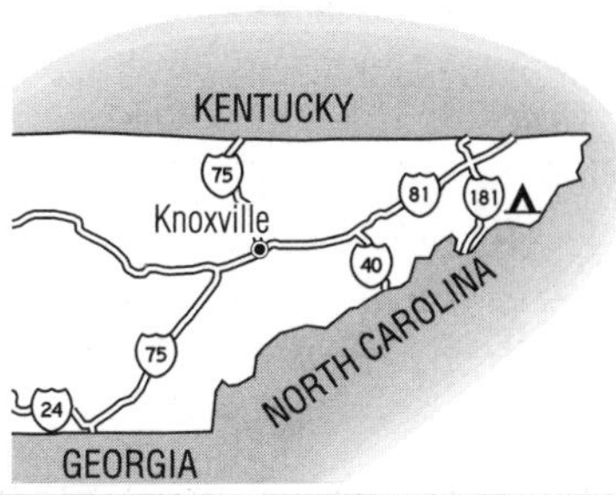

Loop A has ten sites and is designed for RVers. It has large parking areas at each site and electrical hookups are available. Two of the sites are for group camping. Loop B has 13 sites; four of the sites have electricity and are situated closest to Loop A, in an effort to group all of the electricity users together. Loops A and B share a modern bathhouse with flush toilets and warm showers. Loop C is located farthest back in the cove, against a steep hill. It has a very thick understory for maximum privacy. The 13 sites are ideally suited for tent campers. A comfort station with low-volume flush toilets sits in the loop's center. Two campground hosts provide a reassuring air of security.

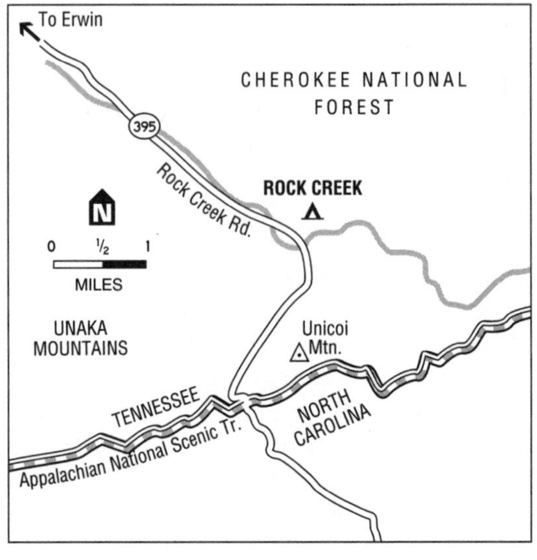

One of the most intriguing features of Rock Creek Recreation Area is the swimming pool. A vestige of the CCC's efforts, the pool is a concrete-and-rock-lined basin of clear stream water, lying behind a small dam. A creek runs into the head of the pool, which is circled by a walkway. A bathhouse with changing rooms, rest rooms, and showers for each sex is nearby. The day was a bit cool for a swim during our visit, but some hardy youngsters were splashing about and having a good time.

Maybe you should save your swim until after a scenic hike in the Unaka Mountain Wilderness that borders the campground. Leave your vehicle at the campsite and depart directly from the campground. The Rattlesnake Ridge Trail (Forest Trail #26) climbs east for 3 miles to the Pleasant Garden Overlook at 4,800 feet. At the base of Unaka Mountain is Rock Creek Falls. FT #26 leads out of the campground along the creek. A few creek crossings later, the multiple descents of the falls come into view beneath the forest canopy—there is always something relaxing about a cascade. This hike is 2.3 miles one way. Other short hikes emanate from the campground. Take the .4-mile Hemlock Forest Trail Loop and find out about this important component of the Southern Appalachian woodlands. Then walk the .2-mile Trail of the Hardwoods Loop for comparison's sake.

Bicyclists have the .8-mile Rock Creek Bicycle Trail to enjoy as well. For any supplies you may need, Erwin is less than four miles away. However, at Rock Creek Campground and the Unaka Wilderness, it feels like civilization is light years away.

To get there, from Erwin take TN 395 east for 3.1 miles. Turn left into the Rock Creek Recreation Area. The campground will be on your right.

KEY INFORMATION

Rock Creek Campground
1205 North Main Street
Erwin, TN 37650

Operated by: U.S. Forest Service

Information: (423) 743-4452

Open: May 1 to October 7

Individual sites: 37

Each site has: Tent pad, lantern post, picnic table, fire pit

Site assignment: First come, first served; no reservations

Registration: Self-registration on site

Facilities: Piped water, warm showers, flush toilets, swimming pool

Parking: At individual sites

Fee: $5 per night; $10 per night with electricity

Elevation: 2,350 feet

Restrictions:

Pets—On leash only

Fires—In fire rings only

Alcoholic beverages—Prohibited

Vehicles—None

Other—14-day stay limit

ROUND MOUNTAIN CAMPGROUND

Newport, Tennessee

Round Mountain Campground is off the beaten path in a seemingly forgotten corner of the Bald Mountains in Cherokee National Forest. Maybe it is the tortuously twisting gravel road that keeps visitation minimal up there. We stayed there on a Friday night with good weather in mid-June and only 3 of the 16 sites were occupied. The three other groups were tent campers. Those who find Round Mountain will relish the tranquil high-country campground so in tune with the woods that it seems to have been constructed by Mother Nature.

The sites of Round Mountain are intermittently located on a single, thickly forested loop road that is bordered in moss—you are literally in the woods. Tall trees, including high-elevation species such as yellow birch and pin cherry, intermingle with hemlock and white pine to provide a thick overhead canopy, shading all campers and the loop road. Junglesque growth of rhododendron on the forest floor buffers campers from one another. Noisy little streams cascade down the mountainside amid the brush.

The first two campsites are actually located on the approach road to the loop. The next five sites are placed where possible between large trees and dense undergrowth. You must climb some steps to reach the campground's most isolated site. One other walk-up site is available. The

CAMPGROUND RATINGS

Beauty:	★★★★★
Site privacy:	★★★★★
Site spaciousness:	★★★★★
Quiet:	★★★★★
Security:	★★★★
Cleanliness/upkeep:	★★★★★

The must-see mountain meadow of Max Patch and lofty, wooded camping await those willing to tackle the long and winding gravel access road.

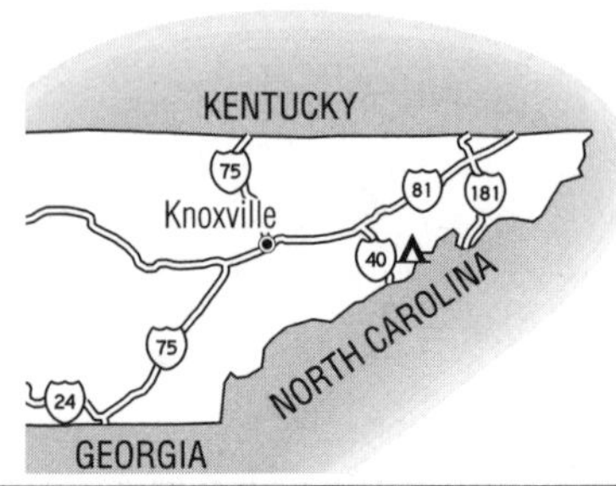

additional sites lie along the loop where they blend in with the scenery, keeping plenty of distance between each other for maximum privacy. A traditional hand-pump well emits cool mountain water. The pump is located at the beginning of the loop, along with a comfort station with clean vault toilets for each sex. Make your last supply stop in Newport and don't plan on coming off Round Mountain until your stay is over. That winding road to and from civilization is a bear.

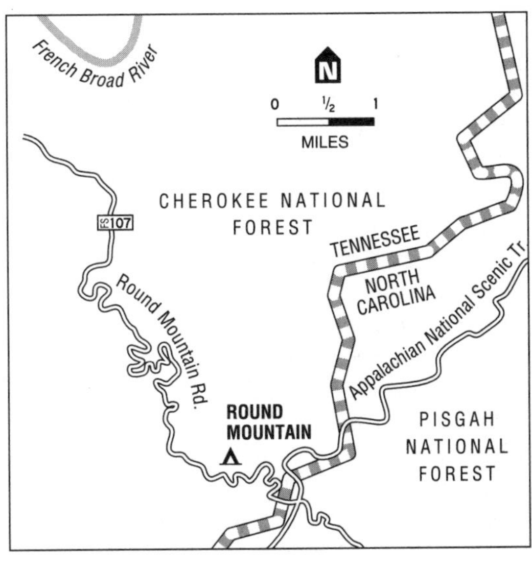

It is just a short distance from the campground to the Walnut Mountain Trail. Walk out to Forest Service Road 107, then go downhill 30 yards to reach the trailhead. It leads 1 mile to Rattlesnake Gap and another mile to the Appalachian Trail near the Walnut Mountain shelter. Attractive scenery is a safe bet either way you turn on the AT from there.

Our June journey took place on a cool mountain morning. Sunlight penetrated the forest canopy here and there, illuminating a light mist that rose from the woodland floor. The famed Max Patch was waiting. We turned left out of the campground on FS 107, motoring 2 miles up to Lemon Gap and the North Carolina border. Naturally, the Appalachian Trail threaded through these lovely groves, as it does in so many of the Southern Appalachians' treasure spots. On we drove, veering right at Lemon Gap on FS 1182 and driving 3.5 miles farther, past a trout pond maintained by the Pisgah National Forest. Old-timers in overalls lounged in lawn chairs beside poles with lines piercing the pond.

Beyond the pond, the forest opened to our left, revealing Max Patch in all its glory. The 230-acre field was once part of a working farm; the field now supports only wildflowers, which bloomed by the thousands, all facing the morning sun. We crested the top of the field at 4,629 feet and were rewarded with a 360-degree view. To the south stood the Great Smoky Mountains. Mount Sterling, with its metal fire tower, and Mount Cammerer, with its distinctive stone tower, stood out among the countless peaks. The open fields of the Bald Mountains stretched out to the north. It seemed as if we were in the very heart of the Southern Appalachians. We may have been.

Round Mountain is my favorite campground in this entire guidebook. Between the quiet solitude and classic, high-country atmosphere of each campsite and the magnificence of Max Patch, this area exudes the best of the uplands that extend from the North Woods into Dixie. After all, it is hard to go wrong combining the beauty of the Appalachians and the charm of the South.

To get there, from Newport take U.S. 25/70 for 10 miles to TN 107 at Del Rio. Turn right on TN 107 and follow it for 5.8 miles. Turn left on gravel FS 107 (Round Mountain Road) as it climbs Round Mountain. After 6 miles, Round Mountain Campground will be on your left.

KEY INFORMATION

Round Mountain Campground
124 Austin Street, Suite #3
Greeneville, TN 37743

Operated by: U.S. Forest Service

Information: (423) 638-4109

Open: May 15 to December 15

Individual sites: 16

Each site has: Tent pad, fire grate, lantern post, picnic table, stand-up grill

Site assignment: First come, first served; no reservations

Registration: Self-registration on site

Facilities: Hand-pumped water, vault toilets

Parking: At campsites only

Fee: $6 per night

Elevation: 3,000 feet

Restrictions:

Pets—On 6-foot leash only

Fires—In fire grates only

Alcoholic beverages—At campsites only

Vehicles—22-foot trailer limit

Other—14-day stay limit

SYLCO CAMPGROUND

Benton, Tennessee

CAMPGROUND RATINGS

Beauty:	★★★★
Site privacy:	★★★★
Site spaciousness:	★★★★★
Quiet:	★★★★★
Security:	★★
Cleanliness/upkeep:	★★★★

Sylco, near the Big Frog and Cohutta wildernesses, is the most primitive campground in this entire guidebook.

If you place a high priority on quiet solitude and close-at-hand wilderness hiking, Sylco is just the place for you. It is located in an isolated area of the Cherokee National Forest in the extreme southeastern corner of Tennessee. You don't have to worry about RVs or trailers coming to this campground. There are three ways to get in here and each way is rough and remote, just like the Sylco area. Then out of nowhere, in the middle of nowhere, appears a grassy plot of land interspersed with shade trees and picnic tables! Just make sure you have your supplies with you.

Primarily used as a hunting camp in fall, this campground is very lightly used the rest of the year. It is so lightly used that the Forest Service doesn't even charge campers to stay here! And only a few of the 12 sites appear to get enough use to even beat down the grass that grows around the picnic tables.

It's remote—no registration and no campground hosts. Some sites don't even have both a picnic table and grill; some just have a fire ring with the table. There's even one grill with no table. You'll find no tent pads either. Just pitch your tent right on the grass; it may slope a bit. This is the most primitive campground in this guidebook. Not to say this place is ragged and neglected; it's just remote—and clean.

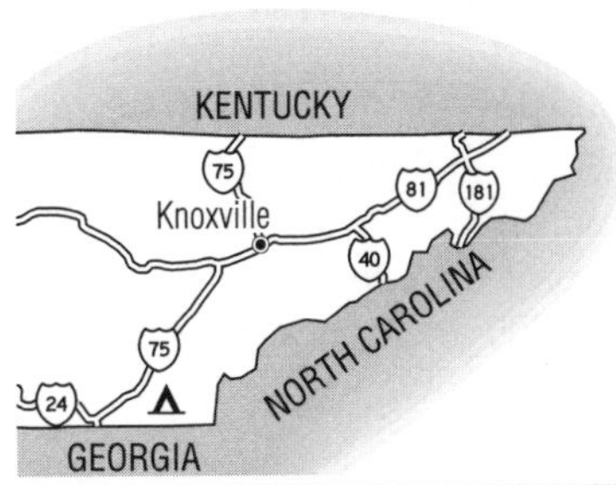

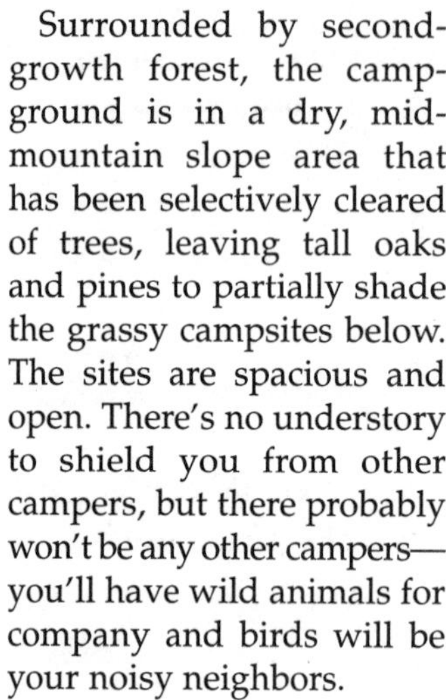

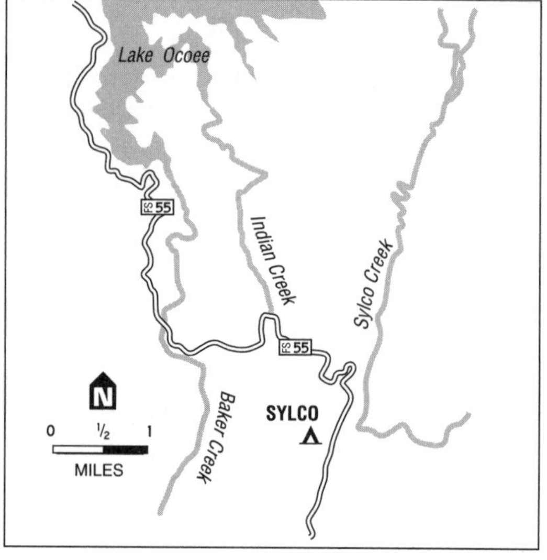

Surrounded by second-growth forest, the campground is in a dry, mid-mountain slope area that has been selectively cleared of trees, leaving tall oaks and pines to partially shade the grassy campsites below. The sites are spacious and open. There's no understory to shield you from other campers, but there probably won't be any other campers—you'll have wild animals for company and birds will be your noisy neighbors.

This lightly used campground extends onto both sides of the road. A short loop swings by the four sites on the downslope. Their tables are fairly close together, so the sites could be suitable for a group camp. A larger loop circles around the upper eight sites. All but one of the sites are in the center of the loop. None of the sites have an official parking spur. Pull over to one side of the loop or just park in the grass. Only two of the sites appear to have been used in recent years and they have parking areas. A vault toilet for each sex stands at the high point of the upper loop.

The campground has no Forest Service–provided water. But nature will provide you with some in case you left yours behind. A narrow path leads 75 yards downslope from the lowest picnic table of the lower loop to a small clear stream. To be on the safe side, treat or boil this water.

Sylco makes a great base camp for the area's wilderness hiking, trout and smallmouth bass fishing, and forest drives. But you'll need a Forest Service map of the Cherokee to make your way around. Big Frog and Cohutta form a 45,000-acre wilderness area (plenty of room for a bear or two). Three miles south of Sylco is Jacks River and the Cohutta Wilderness in Georgia. The

Jacks River Trail (Forest Trail #13) follows an old railroad bed, crossing Jacks River many times. Look for rotting crossties and old railroad spikes. Trout and some especially aggressive smallmouth bass dwell here. The 8-mile hike to Jacks River Falls is worth the 20 fords.

If you like the view from up high, take one of the trails that lead to the top of Big Frog Mountain (4,224 feet), centerpiece of the Big Frog Wilderness. Take the Chestnut Mountain Trail (FT #63) and climb the mountain connecting the Wolf Ridge Trail for a 3.7-mile hike to the mountaintop. Another fine route uses Big Creek Trail (FT #68) connecting to Barkleggin Trail, then to Big Frog via Big Frog Trail. Big Creek offers quality trout fishing as well.

Excellent forest drives can be used to loop back to Sylco. No four-wheel-drive vehicles are necessary. Peavine Road (Forest Service Road 221) leads back to U.S. 64 and the famed Ocoee River. Big Frog Road (FS 62) skirts Big Frog and Cohutta wildernesses offering a taste of the wild without leaving your vehicle. Go slow, ignore the bumps, and try to keep your eyes on the road as well as the scenery.

To get there, from Benton drive south on U.S. 411 2 miles to U.S. 64. Take U.S. 64 east for 6 miles to the Ocoee District Ranger Station. Buy a map of the Cherokee National Forest! From the Ranger Station, take U.S. 64 west for 4.9 miles. Turn left on Cookson Creek/ Baker's Creek Road for 3.5 miles to national forest boundary; at boundary, Baker's Creek Road becomes FS 55. Continue on FS 55 for 6.5 miles to Sylco.

KEY INFORMATION

Sylco Campground
Route 1, Box 348D
Benton, TN 37307

Operated by: U.S. Forest Service

Information: (423) 338-5201

Open: Year-round

Individual sites: 12

Each site has: Picnic table, grill

Site assignment: First come, first served; no reservations

Registration: Not necessary

Facilities: Vault toilet

Parking: At campsites

Fee: None

Elevation: 1,200 feet

Restrictions:

Pets—On leash only

Fires—In fire rings only

Alcoholic beverages—At campsites only

Vehicles—None

NORTH CAROLINA CAMPGROUNDS

NORTH CAROLINA

BIG CREEK CAMPGROUND

Cove Creek, North Carolina

The Great Smoky Mountains National Park has a somewhat undeserved reputation of being overcrowded. Sure, some places can seem a bit peopled, but if you know the right places to go, your limited time in the park can be a relaxing getaway. Big Creek Campground is one of those places. It is the Smokies' smallest campground and its sole tent-only campground. This walk-in campground is set deep in the woods adjacent to the pure mountain waters of Big Creek—so deep, in fact, that when you come to the campground parking area you'll wonder where the campground is. For your information, it's between the campground parking area and noisy Big Creek.

A small footpath leaves the parking area and loops the 12 campsites in the shade of tall hardwoods. Since it's a walk-in campground, you must tote your camping supplies anywhere from 100 to 300 feet. But after that, you'll be hearing only the intonations of Big Creek and smelling the wildflowers, rather than hearing a Chevy engine and smelling exhaust fumes, as all cars are left behind in the common parking area.

Five of the sites are directly creekside. Each site is spacious enough to spread your gear about. The new tent pads are elevated and well drained. A somewhat sparse understory reduces privacy, but the intimate walk-in setup magnifies an

CAMPGROUND RATINGS

Beauty:	★★★★
Site privacy:	★★★
Site spaciousness:	★★★★
Quiet:	★★★★★
Security:	★★★★
Cleanliness/upkeep:	★★★★

Only tents are allowed at this walk-in campground located in the Smokies' remote "Far East."

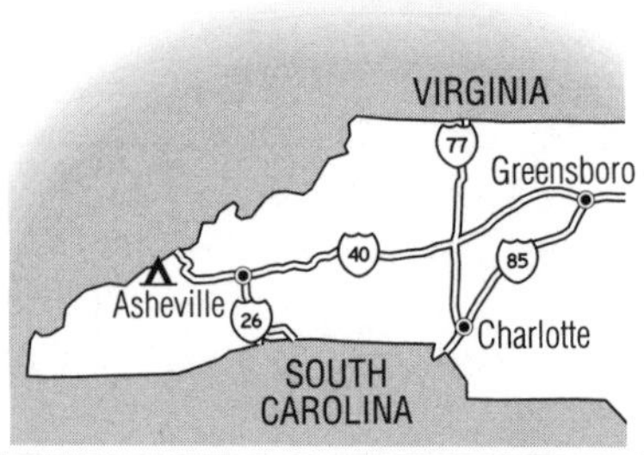

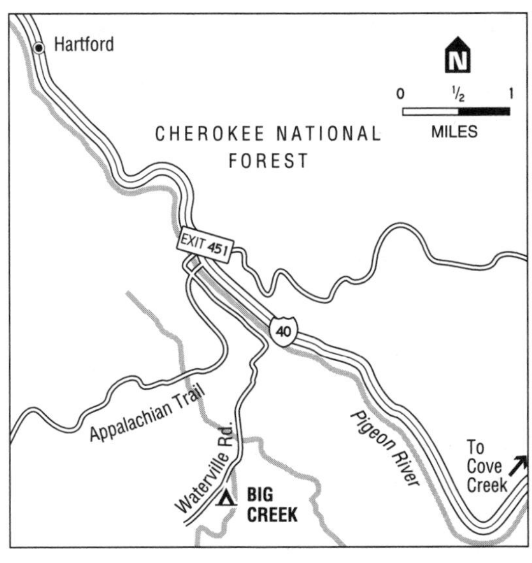

atmosphere of camaraderie among fellow campers not necessarily found in larger drive-in campgrounds.

The campground comfort station borders the parking area. It houses flush toilets for each sex and a large sink with a cold water faucet. Two other water spigots are situated along the footpath loop. A recycling bin is located in the parking area. A pay phone is located one mile back down the gravel road at the Big Creek Ranger Station. Limited supplies can be acquired a bit farther down Big Creek at Mountain Momma's Country Store, but try to bring in what you need. That way you can spend your time enjoying the park. And Big Creek is a great base for that.

The Big Creek Trail starts at the campground. It traces an old railroad grade from the logging era. Cool off the old-fashioned way in one of the many swimming holes that pool up between the white rapids of Big Creek. Gaze up the sides of the valley; the rock bluffs you see have sheltered Smokies wayfarers in days gone by. Hike 3.3 miles up Big Creek and find the tumbling cascades of Mouse Creek Falls. Falls often occur where a feeder creek enters a main stream. The main stream valley erodes faster than the side stream valley, creating a hanging side canyon and then a waterfall. Continue on to Walnut Bottoms at 5 miles. This area has historically had more man–bear encounters than anywhere in the park; don't stray too far from your food. Crestmont Logging Company once had a camp here in the early 1900s, but now the area has returned to its former splendor. Three other trails splinter from Walnut Bottoms if you wish to explore more.

How about a strenuous hike through old-growth forest to a mountaintop capped in a Canadian-type forest with a 360-degree view from a fire tower? It's 6 miles up the Baxter Creek Trail, but your efforts will be amply rewarded. Start at the Big Creek picnic area just below the campground and go for it. Or take the Mount Sterling Trail from Mount Sterling Gap on nearby NC 284. It's only 3 miles to the tower this way. Just up from the Big Creek Ranger Station is the Chestnut Branch Trail. It leads 2 miles to the highest and wildest section of the entire Appalachian Trail, which traverses the Smoky Mountains. The historic fire tower at Mount Cammerer is only 4 miles farther. Or loop back on the AT to Davenport Gap and road walk a short piece back to the campground.

Big Creek is wilderness tent camping at its best. The walk-in setting is your first step into the natural world of the Smokies. The rest of your adventure is limited only by your desire to explore the 500,000 acres in Big Creek Campground's backyard.

To get there, from Cove Creek take I-40 west for 15 miles, crossing the Tennessee state line, to the Waterville exit, #451. Cross the Pigeon River, then turn left to follow the Pigeon upstream. Come to an intersection 2.3 miles after crossing the Pigeon. Proceed forward through the intersection and soon enter the park. Pass the Big Creek Ranger Station and drive to the end of the gravel road and the campground after 3.5 miles.

KEY INFORMATION

Big Creek Campground
Star Route 72
Newport, TN 37821

Operated by: Great Smoky Mountains National Park

Information: (423) 436-1228

Open: May 1 to October 31

Individual sites: 12

Each site has: Picnic table, fire pit, lantern post

Site assignment: First come, first served; no reservations

Registration: Self-registration

Facilities: Flush toilets, cold running water

Parking: At individual sites

Fee: $6 per night

Elevation: 1,700 feet

Restrictions:

Pets—On leash only

Fires—In fire pits only

Alcoholic beverages—At campsite only

Vehicles—No RVs, tents only

Other—7-day stay limit

NORTH CAROLINA

BLACK MOUNTAIN CAMPGROUND

Burnsville, North Carolina

Black Mountain Campground has been around a long time. Over the years it has been taken care of well. Now it is like an antique, treasured by families that have been returning to Black Mountain through the generations. They come here to enjoy the relaxed country atmosphere in a forested setting that offers a sampling of the wild country in the shadow of the Black Mountains.

Cross the South Toe River on a wide bridge and enter Black Mountain Campground. To your right is a gravel road with a turnaround at the end. One of two campground hosts resides in a cottage there. This road parallels the Toe and contains 14 heavily wooded sites. Hemlock and rhododendron shroud these sites from one another. The six riverside sites are the most coveted. Two isolated sites are nestled far in the woods at the back of the turnaround.

Two water spigots are located along the road. A comfort station with flush toilets for each sex is situated midway along the road. A caged garbage disposal area lies next to the comfort station. The garbage areas are now caged because Black Mountain Campground once had a big problem with bears. Keep the Black Mountain bears wild and dispose of your trash properly.

The main campground is on an oval road that loops a large field. There are 29 sites on this loop. The 12 sites on the interior of the loop by the field have more

CAMPGROUND RATINGS

Beauty:	★★★
Site privacy:	★★★★
Site spaciousness:	★★★★★
Quiet:	★★★
Security:	★★★★★
Cleanliness/upkeep:	★★★★

The Black River Recreation Area offers a family atmosphere and quality camping in a forested country setting.

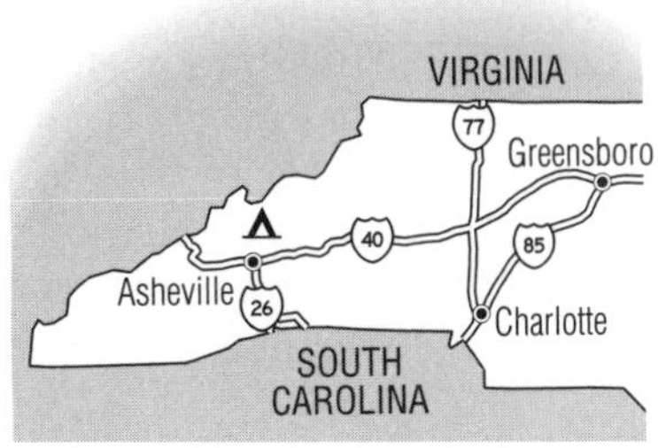

grassy understory beneath tall shade trees. Privacy is sacrificed for the openness of these sites.

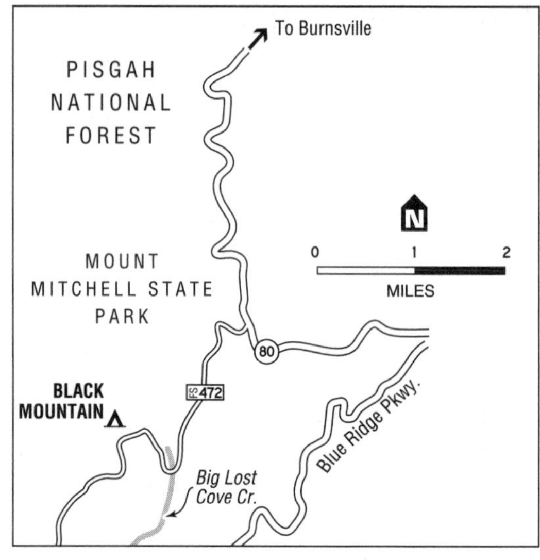

The 17 sites on the exterior of the loop have a denser understory and are pressed against a hill, which required some site leveling. The tree canopy is thicker here, especially on the southwest side of the loop, where a small stream meanders through the rhododendron thickets. Two comfort stations lie at the farthest ends of the loop. Four water spigots make a cool drink easy to come by.

Three other sites are located along the road to the Briar Bottom Group Camp. They are close across the road from the Toe River and have a water spigot of their own. It is a bit of a walk to one of the three comfort stations, though.

Children often play in the field at the main loop's center. A volleyball net was up on my weekday visit, yet the campground was very quiet. However, expect it to fill on summer weekends. Generally, tent campers constitute over two-thirds of the patrons. Adjacent to the main loop is the campground amphitheater. On weekend nights you can expect anything from local gospel groups to bluegrass pickers to ranger programs. The emphasis here is on old-fashioned family fun.

Bicycling, fishing, and hiking are the three most popular outdoor pursuits at Black Mountain Campground. Bring your bike and pedal the Briar Bottom Bicycle Trail. This trail starts at the Briar Bottom Group Campground, parallels the Toe River, and loops back around, crossing two bridges. It returns to the campground at one mile. From the Briar Bottom Trail, you can take a half-mile foot trail to Setrock Creek Falls, a scenic cascade. Another moderate hike is the Devils Den Forest Walk. It begins at the main campground loop and makes a loop of its own during its half-hour woodland stroll.

For the strong-winded, the Green Knob Trail starts across the road from the campground and climbs 3.3 steep miles to a lookout tower at 5,070 feet. This is a strenuous hike. If you really want to check your physical condition, try the Mount Mitchell Trail. It starts near the amphitheater and climbs nearly 3,700 feet to the highest point east of the Mississippi.

The Toe River and its tributaries are well known for their trout fishing. But don't always expect to dip a line right by the campground on summer weekends. At this time, children are often swimming and tubing in the Toe's cool waters as it flows through the campground.

The setting and the activities are among the many reasons families and friends return to Black Mountain Campground again and again. Once you give it a try, you may return again yourself.

To get there, from Burnsville take U.S. 19-E 5 miles, then turn right on NC 80 for 12 miles to FS 472. Turn right on FS 472 for 3 miles. Black Mountain Campground will be on your right.

KEY INFORMATION

Black Mountain Campground
P.O. Box 128
Burnsville, NC 28714

Operated by: Cradle of Forestry Interpretive Association

Information: (704) 682-6146

Open: April 15 to October 31

Individual sites: 46

Each site has: Tent pad, fire ring, picnic table, lantern post

Site assignment: First come, first served; no reservations

Registration: Self-registration on site

Facilities: Flush toilets, piped water, pay phone

Parking: At campsites only

Fee: $10 per night

Elevation: 3,200 feet

Restrictions:

Pets—On a 6-foot leash only

Fires—In fire ring only

Alcoholic beverages—At campsites only

Vehicles—23-foot trailer length limit

Other—14-day stay limit June 1 to September 1

CABLE COVE CAMPGROUND

Fontana Village, North Carolina

Recent history dominates the theme of this charming and sedate campground. It sits on former farmland once tilled by the Cable family. After World War II broke out, the demand for aluminum soared. Nearby, Fontana Dam was built to generate power to produce the aluminum. The farming families moved away and the Forest Service moved in, later establishing a campground in the hollow.

Cable Cove's proximity to Fontana Lake makes it a favorite spot for boaters. It is an ideal camp from which to visit the Smoky Mountains via boat, thus avoiding the auto traffic. Fontana is a lightly used lake, though the views of the park are unlimited and unspoiled by troops of tourists that fill the highways on busy summer weekends.

Cable Cove Campground stretches out along a gravel road that slopes down toward Fontana Lake, half a mile away. A small loop at the end of the campground road enables drivers to turn around; this loop holds five campsites. Cable Creek, a small trout stream, parallels the road on the right. The campground is well maintained, quiet, and unassuming. Shortly after arriving, I felt as if I belonged there, like one of the neighbors.

The ten creekside sites are heavily wooded and have a thick understory. The sites are spacious, yet have an air of privacy due to the junglelike vegetation along Cable Creek. The 11 sites opposite

CAMPGROUND RATINGS

Beauty: ★★★★
Site privacy: ★★★
Site spaciousness: ★★★★★
Quiet: ★★★★
Security: ★★★★
Cleanliness/upkeep: ★★★★

Stay at Cable Cove and access the Smoky Mountains National Park by boat or land, free of traffic hassles.

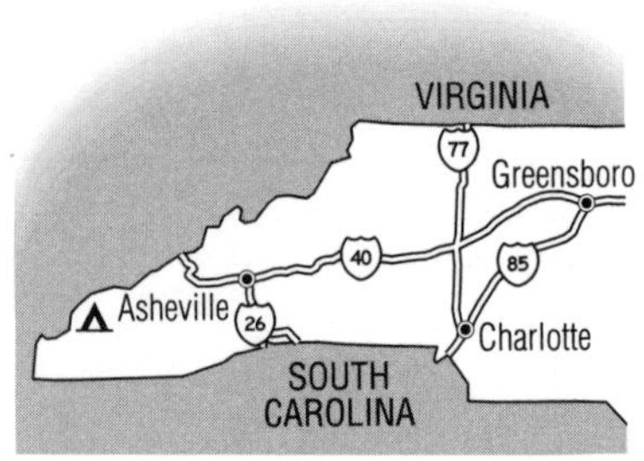

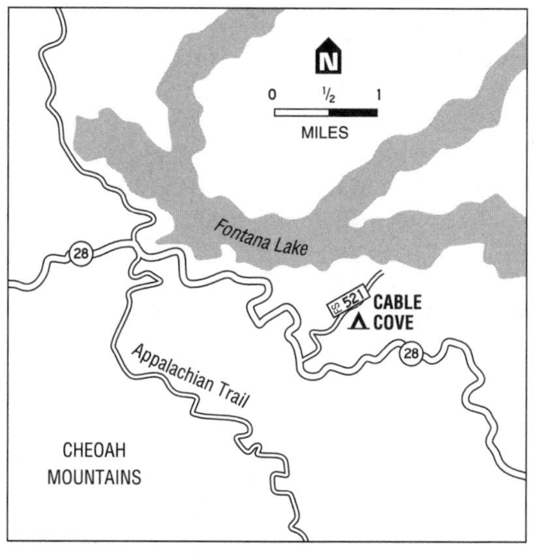

the creek have a grassy gladelike understory beneath second-growth trees reclaiming the old fields. The grass had been freshly trimmed and looked especially attractive during my stay. This "yard" space makes for a more open camping area, one conducive to visiting your neighbor, a customary thing to do in friendly western North Carolina. These campsites are among the largest I have ever seen, extending far back from the road. An area of brush and trees divides the upper and lower campground. Beyond the brush are the five sites at the turn-around loop. These sites lie beneath deep woods adjacent to Cable Creek.

Three water spigots have been placed at even intervals in the linear campground. Two comfort stations with flush toilets for each sex are at either end of the campground; campers in the middle may have to walk a bit to use them. But even this stroll could be an opportunity to get to know your neighbor. We camped toward the middle, and by the time we left the gravel road resembled a country lane, slow-moving and full of good neighbors.

Most of your neighbors will be boaters. A high-quality boat ramp is half a mile away; campers use it to fish for bream, bass, trout, and walleye, as well as to access the Smokies. Using a boat to access the park is a smart way to beat the crowds. Several hiking trails in the Smokies run right down to the lake. Check out the 360-degree view from Shuckstack Fire Tower; the tower is visible from the lake. Boat up the Eagle Creek arm of Fontana Lake. From the embayment, the Lost Cove Trail leads 3 miles up to the Appalachian Trail. Just .4 mile south on the AT is the tower. The outline of Fontana Lake is easily discerned from the tower. Look northeast and see the spine of the Smokies until it fades from view.

Across the water from Cable Cove is the famed Hazel Creek. Its trout waters have been featured in fishing magazines for years. But don't visit just for the fish. Hike up the gentle trail that parallels the creek and discover relics of the Smokies' past, including old homesites, fields, and mining endeavors. Wide bridges spanning Hazel Creek make this walk even more pleasant. You can only access this end of the trail by boat. If you don't have a boat, contact Fontana Marina at (704) 498-2211, ext. 277 to arrange for a shuttle. The marina is only 4 miles west of Cable Cove. You can purchase limited supplies at the small store at Fontana Village Resort near the marina. But you are better off stocking up in Maryville, Tennessee, if you are coming from the Volunteer State, or in Robbinsville, North Carolina, south of Cable Cove on NC 143.

Also near the marina is the engineering marvel that is Fontana Dam, tallest dam east of the Rockies at 480 feet. It is well worth a visit. A Visitor Center recounts the story of the dam, and a cable car will take you down to its powerhouse. You can cross the dam in your auto, which is the landlubber's way to access the Smokies at one of the more remote trailheads. Trace the Appalachian Trail 3.3 miles up to Shuckstack and its tower. Or take the undulating Lakeshore Trail through the Smokies' lush flora 5 miles to Eagle Creek and its embayment. Whether by land or water, this slice of the Smokies is a gem to visit.

KEY INFORMATION

Cable Cove Campground
Route 1, Box 16A
Robbinsville, NC 28771

Operated by: U.S. Forest Service

Information: (704) 479-6431

Open: April 14 to October 31

Individual sites: 26

Each site has: Tent pad, lantern post, picnic table, fire grate

Site assignment: First come, first served; no reservations

Registration: Self-registration on site

Facilities: Piped water, low-volume flush toilet

Parking: At campsites only

Fee: $5 per night

Elevation: 1,800 feet

Restrictions:

Pets—On leash only

Fires—In fire grates only

Alcoholic beverages—At campsites only

Vehicles—None

Other—14-day stay limit

To get there, from Fontana Village take NC 28 east for 4.7 miles. Turn left on FS 521 for 1.5 miles. Cable Cove will be on your right.

CATALOOCHEE CAMPGROUND

Canton, North Carolina

Cataloochee Campground is only the first attractive spot you'll see in this valley of meadows, streams, mountains, and history. The celebrated fishing waters of Cataloochee Creek form one border of the campground, while a small feeder stream forms the other. In between is an attractive flat, canopied with stately white pines and dotted with campsites.

The campground has ideal summer weather: warm days and cool nights. An elevation of 2,600 feet is fairly high for a valley campground with a stream the size of Cataloochee Creek. Cataloochee uses the basic campground design: campsites splintering off a loop road. Six of the sites lie along Cataloochee Creek. A few others border the small feeder stream. All the campsites are roomy and placed where the pines allow. An erratic understory of hemlock and rhododendron leaves site privacy to the luck of which site you draw. The campground host is situated at the campground's entrance for your safety and convenience. Be forewarned: bears are sighted yearly at this campground, so properly store your food and keep the wild in the Smoky Mountain bears.

Most RV campers shy away from this campground because the park service does not recommend that RVs make the long drive over rough gravel roads. Cataloochee does fill up on summer weekends, yet with only 27 sites it doesn't seem

CAMPGROUND RATINGS

Beauty:	★★★★★
Site privacy:	★★★★
Site spaciousness:	★★★★★
Quiet:	★★★★★
Security:	★★★★
Cleanliness/upkeep:	★★★★

There is no easy way into Cataloochee Valley, but its very remoteness and inaccessibility keep it one of the Smokies' best kept and least visited special places.

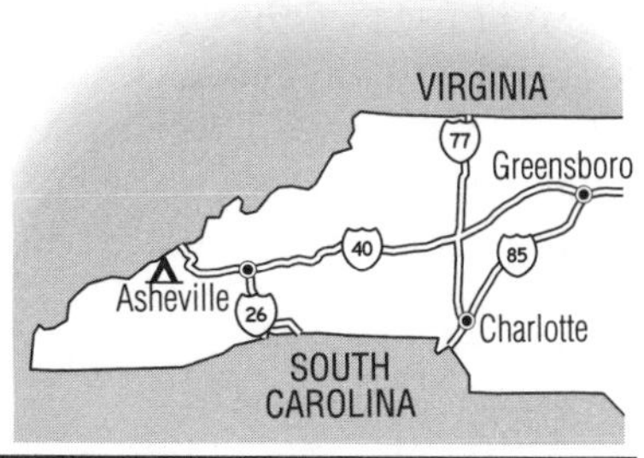

overly crowded. A comfort station is located at the head of the campground next to the campground host. It has flush toilets for each sex and a cold water faucet that pours into a large sink. Another water spigot is at the other end of the campground.

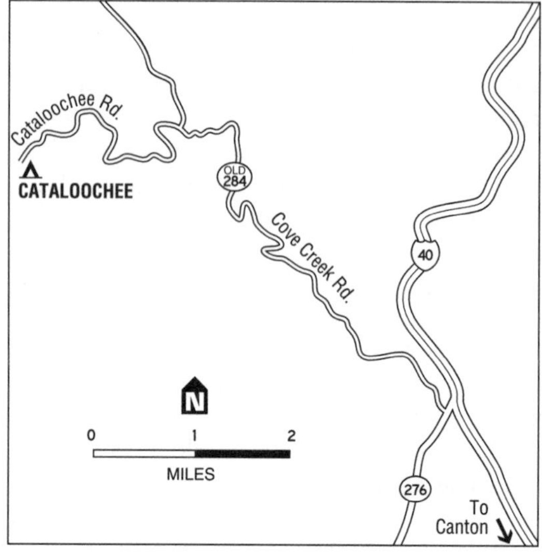

With all there is to do, you probably will only be at the campground to rest from perusing the park. The first order of business is an auto tour of Cataloochee Valley. Get the handy park service pamphlet and gain a feel of the area. An old church, a school, and numerous homesites are a delight to explore. Informative displays explain further about life long ago in this part of the world.

Cataloochee Valley is a hiker's paradise. Take the 7.4-mile undulating Boogerman Trail that loops among old-growth hemlocks and tulip trees while passing through different vegetation zones. Old homesites add a touch of human history; numerous footbridges make exploring this watery mountainland fun and easy on the feet. Or take the Little Cataloochee Trail to Little Cataloochee Church. Set in the backwoods, the church was built in 1890 and is still used today. Other signs of man you'll see are a ramshackle cabin, chimneys, fence posts, and rock walls.

The Cataloochee Divide Trail starts at 4,000 feet and rambles along the ridgeline border that straddles Maggie and Cataloochee valleys. To the north is the rugged green expanse of the national park and to the south are the developed areas along U.S. 19. Grassy knolls along the way make good viewing and relaxing spots.

Using the Rough Fork, Caldwell Fork, and Fork Ridge trails, you can make another loop. Pass the fields of the Woody Place, then climb Fork Ridge, descend to Caldwell Fork, and climb Fork Ridge yet again to experience the literal highs and lows of hiking.

The meadows of Cataloochee Valley are an ideal setting for a picnic. Decide on your favorite view and lay down your blanket. Nearby shady streams will serenade you as you look up at the wooded ridges that line the valley. Deer and other critters feed at the edges of the fields. Dusk is an ideal time to see Cataloochee's wildlife.

Summer weather had finally hit during our campground venture. The air had a lazy, hazy feel as we toured the valley's historic structures. I fished away the afternoon, catching a few rainbows downstream from the campground. After grilling hamburgers for supper, we walked up the Rough Fork Trail to the Woody Place. The homestead looked picturesque as the late-evening sunlight filtered through the nearby forest. As we came back to the trailhead, deer browsed in the Cataloochee meadow. We knew we had come to the right place. So will you.

To get there, from Canton drive 11 miles west on I-40 to Exit 20, then drive west on NC 276. Follow it a short distance, then turn right on Cove Creek Road, which you follow nearly 6 miles to enter the park. Two miles beyond the park boundary, turn left onto the paved Cataloochee Road and follow it 3 miles. The campground will be on your left.

KEY INFORMATION

Cataloochee Campground
Route 2, Box 550
Waynesville, NC 28786

Operated by: Great Smoky Mountains National Park

Information: (423) 436-1228

Open: May to October

Individual sites: 27

Each site has: Picnic table, fire pit, lantern post

Site assignment: First come, first served; no reservations

Registration: Self-registration on site

Facilities: Flush toilets, cold running water

Parking: At individual sites

Fee: $6 per night

Elevation: 2,610 feet

Restrictions:

Pets—On leash only

Fires—In fire pits only

Alcoholic beverages—At campsites only

Vehicles—None

Other—7-day stay limit

CHEOAH POINT CAMPGROUND

Robbinsville, North Carolina

Perched on a hilly peninsula overlooking the blue-green waters of 2,863-acre Santeelah Lake, Cheoah Point Campground is nearly surrounded by water on all sides. Campers may dock their boats and access their campsites from the lake itself. Of course, the most popular way is to drive to your favorite site and put your boat in the water later; the effect is the same. The campsites on this ridgetop loop are literally carved into the hillside beneath a fragrant, open pine-oak forest.

Steps lead down to most campsites on a finger ridge sloping down the lake. The sites are usually paired fairly close together, with a good stretch of woods before the next pair of sites on the next finger ridge. A second set of steps leads down to the lake, effectively accessing the lake. The sites themselves are not directly lakeside; they sit above the lake and provide an eye-pleasing view.

It's difficult to categorize the campsites. Nearly every one has its own unique character. Though the sites were built by the Forest Service, judging by the elaborate site leveling, access paths, wooden stairs, and concrete and stone used to build this campground, the Army Corps of Engineers, or some other engineers, must have helped. It's the most elaborate site work I've ever seen; that's what makes this place so special. The campsites are almost like a playground. The sites located high on the

CAMPGROUND RATINGS

Beauty:	★★★★★
Site privacy:	★★★★
Site spaciousness:	★★★★★
Quiet:	★★★
Security:	★★★★★
Cleanliness/upkeep:	★★★★

See and enjoy Santeelah Lake from Cheoah Point Campground.

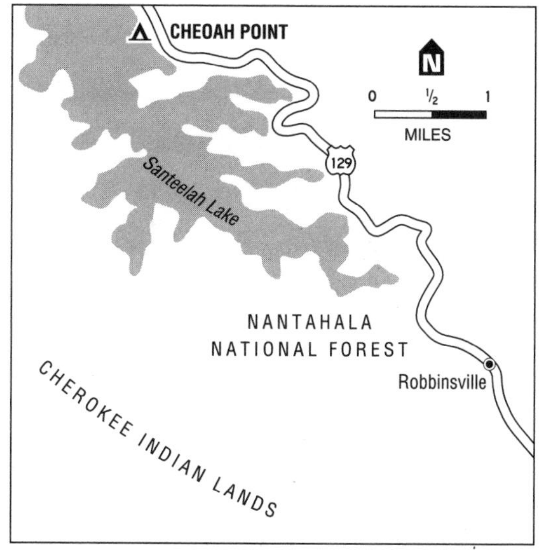

interior of the loop are also designed well, with the added bonus of lake views through the trees.

A campground host is stationed at the ridgetop loop's entrance for camper security. Three water spigots are dispersed amid the airy campsites. Paths lead from the campsites to a central comfort station with low-volume flush toilets for each sex.

Santeelah Lake resulted from the demand for electrical power by the Aluminum Company of America (ALCOA). The Little Tennessee River basin is an area of high rainfall in mountainous country, resulting in high runoff, narrow dam sites, and good reservoir possibilities for the development of hydroelectric power. It also results in clear, picturesque lakes that sparkle beneath the Southern Appalachians. Santeelah Lake provides water regulation for 176 square miles. The reservoir was built in 1928 to provide additional water for the power plant at nearby Cheoah Lake, which has a small reservoir capacity. A 5-mile pressure tunnel leads over and through the mountains, feeding water to Cheoah Lake. Currently, the Tennessee Valley Authority (TVA) and ALCOA work hand-in-hand to provide power for the ALCOA plant in Alcoa, Tennessee, and for customers in the TVA region.

The Forest Service has a nearby boat ramp located just north of the campground. Here you can launch your boat and indulge in your favorite water sports—if you can keep your head focused on the water instead of the scenery around you. Fishing is popular; bass, trout, and bream call Santeelah home. Waterskiing and swimming are favorite summer activities for those trying to escape the heat. The scenery helps make this lakeside campground special. So often in the Southern Appalachians you view lakes from the mountaintops; Santeelah Lake offers a perspective of the mountains from the lake.

If you like to keep at least one foot on the ground, try hiking the Wauchecha Bald Trail. It starts across from the campground entrance and travels a rugged 7.1 miles to the Wauchecha Bald Lookout. It used to be called the Old Roughy Trail, so be prepared for some tough hiking. No matter how much of this trail you hike, when you return you'll be ready for a dip in the cool waters of Santeelah Lake.

Supplies of all kinds at reasonable prices can be found in Robbinsville, a mountain town not yet caught up in the tourist frenzy. My Jeep was towed there once after a four-wheeling mishap, requiring major auto work. I was treated fairly and, consequently, have always had a good feeling about the place. Recent excursions there have confirmed my initial feelings about Robbinsville.

To get there, from Robbinsville take U.S. 129 north for 7 miles. Turn left at the sign, go .8 mile. The campground will be on your right.

KEY INFORMATION

Cheoah Point Campground
Route 1, Box 16-A
Robbinsville, NC 28771

Operated by: U.S. Forest Service

Information: (704) 479-6431

Open: April 15 to October 31

Individual sites: 26

Each site has: Tent pad, fire grate, picnic table, lantern post

Site assignment: First come, first served; no reservations

Registration: Self-registration on site

Facilities: Piped water, flush toilets

Parking: At individual sites

Fee: $5 per night

Elevation: 1,950 feet

Restrictions:

Pets—On leash only

Fires—In fire grates only

Alcoholic beverages—At campsites only

Vehicles—None

Other—14-day stay limit

DAVIDSON RIVER CAMPGROUND

Brevard, North Carolina

Davidson River Campground is centrally located in the heart of the Southern Highlands region of North Carolina. The 161 sites qualify Davidson as large, but eight separate camping loops spread campers over a surprisingly sizable and level area alongside the Davidson River. This layout makes the campground appear less bustling than it really is. Davidson River attracts everyone from tent campers to some RV enthusiasts.

Water spigots and comfort stations with hot showers and flush toilets are conveniently located at each loop. Davidson has a variety of campsites: wooded, riverside sites; open, grassy sites; sites beneath hardwood trees; and sites carpeted with pine needles. All the sites share a well-landscaped appearance.

Just across from the campground is the Pisgah District Ranger Station. Purchase a map of the area and it will pay for itself in time saved pursuing your recreational opportunities. Helpful staffers oversee the center and will gladly answer your questions.

Davidson has few vacant sites during summer. That's not surprising with so much to do in the area. Nearby is the mountain town of Brevard, host of Festival of the Arts Week and the renown Brevard Music Festival. We relaxed at a coffee shop, then toured the art and gift stores and quaint antique malls of the downtown

CAMPGROUND RATINGS

Beauty: ★★★★
Site privacy: ★★★
Site spaciousness: ★★★★★
Quiet: ★★★
Security: ★★★★★
Cleanliness/upkeep: ★★★★

At the edge of the Pisgah National Forest, Davidson River Campground provides a good base for exploring the woods and countryside of Transylvania County.

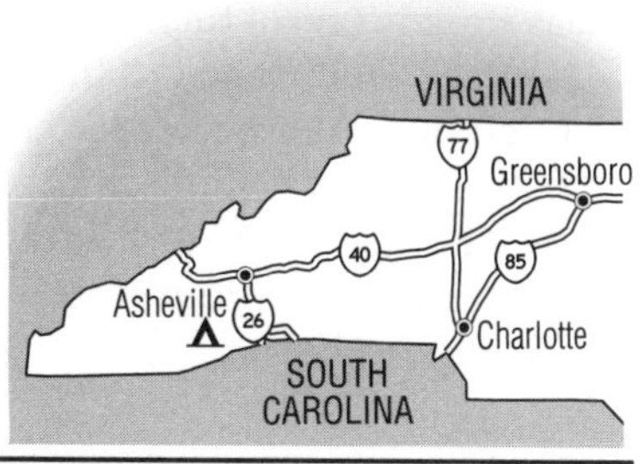

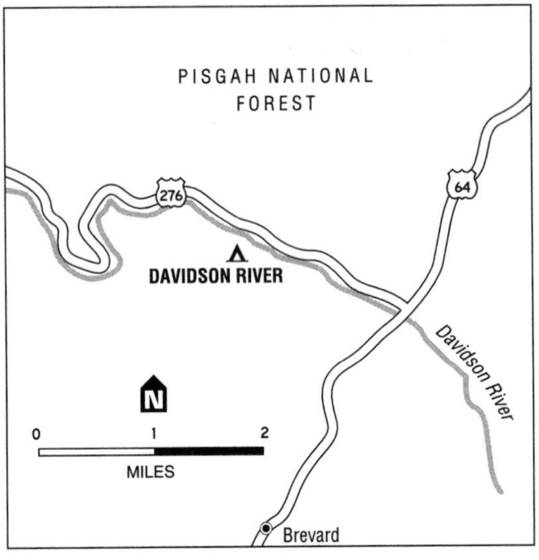

area. Southern cuisine is featured at many of the fine restaurants in town. A burgh of only 6,000, Brevard has a small-town feel, yet it offers virtually all of the supplies that a camper would need.

Davidson River Campground is located in Transylvania County. *Transylvania* means "across the woods." Hikers need not leave the campground to make their own woodland travels. The North Slope Trail begins just past the main campground entrance. This 4.5-mile loop ascends a rich cove to a ridgetop, then descends along the Davidson River. The Art Loeb National Recreation Trail starts on the left of the campground entrance road. It climbs up to and along Shut-in Ridge. At 3.3 miles, the trail intersects a half-mile connector trail linking the Art Loeb Trail with the North Slope Trail, making another loop possible. The Exercise Trail starts in the campground, too. It's a 1.5-mile, well-graded loop for easy walking or jogging. It passes the old English Chapel and through the woods along the Davidson River.

Pisgah National Forest is famous for its granite-domed mountains. Looking Glass Rock is one of them, accessible by the fairly strenuous 3.1-mile Looking Glass Rock Trail. To get to the trailhead, drive 3.5 miles west on U.S. 276 and turn left on Forest Service Road 475. The Looking Glass Trail begins .4 mile on the right. You'll climb through hemlock and mountain laurel then come to the front of the dome at 2.7 miles. Keep ascending for another .4 mile to the top of the dome. To your west is the Blue Ridge Parkway. The Pisgah stretches out in all directions.

Like to fish? Nearby streams are stocked with trout by the Pisgah North Carolina State Fish Hatchery, one of the largest in the East. Three other watery features are nearby: Moore Cove Falls, Looking Glass Falls, and the family favorite, Sliding Rock. Four miles west on U.S. 276 is Looking Glass Falls. Steps lead down to the pool created by the unbroken rush of water dropping some 60 feet.

One mile west of Looking Glass Falls on U.S. 276 is the Moore Cove Trail. Descend along Moore Branch for .6 mile and come to the 45-foot cascades of Moore Cove Falls. One mile west of Moore Cove Trail on U.S. 276 is Sliding Rock. This is a popular and developed swimming hole centered around a natural water slide. Water lovers glide 60 feet down the cool waters of Looking Glass Creek into a seven-foot-deep pool. A site attendant, on duty from Memorial Day to mid-August, oversees the area, which is complete with rest rooms, changing area, large parking area, and observation deck. This alcohol-free zone allows family fun on hot summer days.

To get there, from Brevard take U.S. 64 East for 3.5 miles. Turn left on U.S. 276 for 1.3 miles. Davidson River Campground will be on your left across the river.

KEY INFORMATION

Davidson River Campground
P.O. Box 8
Pisgah Forest, NC 28768

Operated by: Cradle of Forestry Interpretive Association

Information: (704) 877-3265

Open: Year-round

Individual sites: 161

Each site has: Tent pad, picnic table, fire grate, lantern post

Site assignment: First come, first served but reservations recommended; reserve up to 7 days in advance by calling (800) 280-2267

Registration: At the gatehouse in summer; self-registration on site rest of year

Facilities: Flush toilets, dump station, water spigots, hot showers

Parking: At campsites only

Fee: $11 per night

Elevation: 2,000 feet

Restrictions:

Pets—On a 6-foot leash only

Fires—In fire rings only

Alcoholic beverages—At campsites only

Vehicles—None

Other—Maximum 30 days total use between Memorial Day and Labor Day

DOUGHTON CAMPGROUND

Sparta, North Carolina

The National Park Service does a really good job with this Blue Ridge Parkway campground. It is located on the crest of the Blue Ridge and has a mountaintop ambience. A smart design spreads out 100-plus sites and makes the area seem like several small campgrounds. Dividing the tent and RV sites into separate sections makes it even better.

The 6,430-acre park and campground are named after former North Carolina Congressman "Muley Bob" Doughton, who fought hard to make the Blue Ridge Parkway become the scenic reality it is. He would be proud of this area that integrates modern structures into the historic dwellings and hiking trails that lace the park.

Before you explore Doughton Park, pick a campsite. It may take a few minutes, as Doughton Campground has six distinct camping areas. It is a generally open, airy campground that is tastefully landscaped and well integrated into the ridgetop setting. Even the most discriminating tent campers will find a site to suit their tastes.

The first loop holds 22 sites and is heavily wooded, yet with a light understory. The sites undulate along a hill and are fairly close, so you may be a tad close to your neighbor. The comfort station is a ways down a sloping path, possibly a little farther than some are willing to walk.

CAMPGROUND RATINGS

Beauty: ★★★★
Site privacy: ★★★
Site spaciousness: ★★★
Quiet: ★★★
Security: ★★★★
Cleanliness/upkeep: ★★★★★

Doughton Campground is much more than a way station along the Blue Ridge Parkway. Explore some of the parkway's finest scenery, then return to your inviting highland campground.

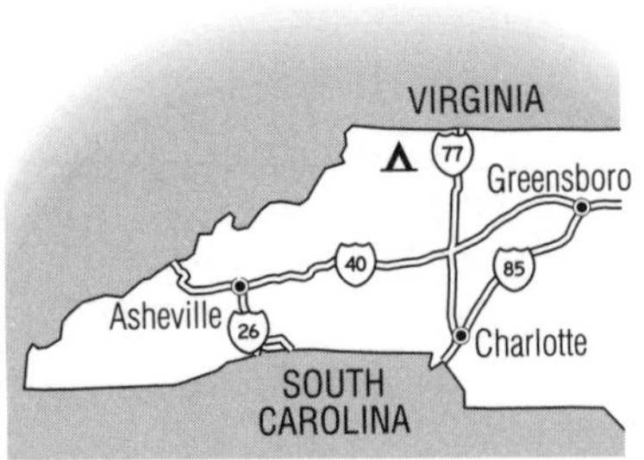

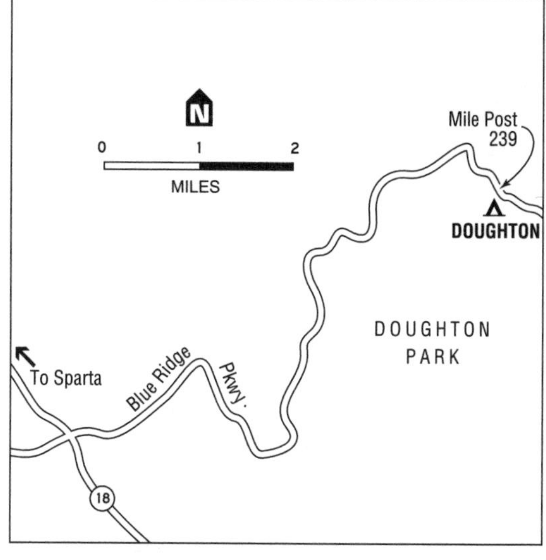

Sites 23–33 are set back in the woods, down from the paved campground road. Short paths lead back to these sites, so you will have to carry your gear to your site. This distance allows for the most rustic camping experience, out of sight from vehicles. The sites closest to the parking area border a grassy field adjacent to the parking area. Campers share the comfort station with the first loop via a short, paved path.

The second loop circles the highest point of the campground. It has 30 sites and is centered with a grassy glade where a water tank sits. Oddly enough, a campsite is located right by the water tank. When I checked it out, I found the view of the surrounding mountain lands worth the intrusion of the green structure. Other sites up there offer intermittent views of the Blue Ridge and beyond. You even have a view from the comfort station at the loop's center.

The main loop continues along the ridge and passes a few sites for larger pop-up tent campers, then enters the campfire circle loop. It has nine sites located in an attractive meadow. Trees have been strategically planted by each campsite for shade and aesthetic appeal.

Beyond the campfire circle loop is yet another loop winding amid hilly forestland. This loop rolls and dips between rock outcrops, with sites tastefully integrated where the land allows. There are 20 sites here. Since it is at the very back of the campground, you will have the least amount of vehicles casually driving by to their respective sites. A comfort station is centered on this loop as well.

Back on the main loop, in an open area backed against woodland, are 11 more sites for larger pop-ups. There is a curious lack of faucets for such a large campground; there are only six and they could have been better placed. But this is a minor inconvenience for such a well-kept and secure campground that is 90% tenters. A campground host lives on site.

The Blue Ridge Parkway is an exercise in scenic beauty, but I think this particular area is exceptional even for the BRP. A drive in either direction will satiate your taste for dramatic landscapes and historic sites. The Brinegar Cabin is just a short distance north. Of course, the most rewarding views are those earned with a little sweat. Doughton Park has over 30 miles of trails that meander through pastures, along wooded ridges, and by mountain streams.

The Bluff Mountain Trail departs from the campground and gives you a sampling of this country. It extends for 3 or so miles in each direction. The Fodderstack Trail climbs to the Wildcat Rocks Overlook and is a 2-mile round-trip. Another recommended trail is Basin Creek, which ends at the Caudill Cabin. This cabin is only accessible by foot. Cedar Ridge Trail begins at the Brinegar Cabin and drops down to Basin Creek. Before you hike any of these trails, stop at the campground hut and pick up a free trail map. Get out there and stretch your legs after enjoying that fantastic Blue Ridge Parkway scenery.

To get there, take NC 18 west from Sparta for 14 miles to the Blue Ridge Parkway. Turn north on the BRP, drive 6 miles to milepost 239. Doughton Park Campground will be on your left.

KEY INFORMATION

Doughton Campground
200 BB & T Building, One Pack Square
Asheville, NC 28801

Operated by: National Park Service

Information: (704) 298-0398

Open: May 1 to October 31

Individual sites: 107

Each site has: Tent pad, fire ring, picnic table

Site assignment: First come, first served; no reservations

Registration: At campground hut

Facilities: Flush toilets, piped water, pay phone

Parking: At campsites only

Fee: $10 per night

Elevation: 3,900 feet

Restrictions:

Pets—On 6-foot leash

Fires—In fire rings only

Alcoholic beverages—At campsites only

Vehicles—None

Other—14-day stay limit; 30-day total limit for calendar year

HANGING DOG CAMPGROUND

Murphy, North Carolina

When people think of Smoky Mountain Country, they picture rolling mountains, deep forests, and rushing streams. That's what comes natural. However, when the white man came here, he started the unnatural job of building dams. The hilly terrain of the Southern Appalachians proved to be fertile ground for creating lakes, and now we have an abundance of scenic lakes that seemingly have mountains growing right out of them. Much of the land around these lakes is owned by you and me, courtesy of the U.S. Forest Service. Along some lakes, the Forest Service has built campgrounds that enable us to enjoy some of these bodies of water. Hanging Dog Campground is just such a place.

Hanging Dog is an unusual name for a campground. It is named after a nearby creek of the same name that flows through a parcel of the neighboring Cherokee Reservation. Legend has it that a brave dog was accidentally snared in the creek while chasing a deer to provide meat for the hungry people. The dog survived and the people named the area to commemorate the canine's actions.

Hanging Dog Campground features four widely separated loops. Each loop is almost like its own campground. A dry pine-oak forest covers the peninsula that borders Hiwassee Lake. Adequate, yet

CAMPGROUND RATINGS

Beauty:	★★★★
Site privacy:	★★★★
Site spaciousness:	★★★★
Quiet:	★★★
Security:	★★★★
Cleanliness/upkeep:	★★★★

Hanging Dog sits by picturesque Hiwassee Lake, nestled in the rural mountains of western North Carolina.

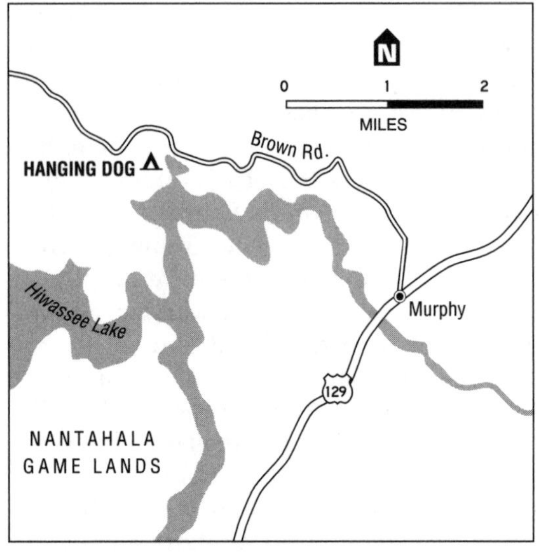

sparse, water supplies and comfort stations are placed in every loop.

This Civilian Conservation Corps–era campground has aged well. Vegetation has been cultivated over the years for the best campground aesthetics. Time moves slowly in this relaxed atmosphere. Adults, who first visited Hanging Dog as children, pass on the joys of camping here to the next generation.

Loop A spurs off to the right of the main campground road. It circles a hollow formed by a tiny stream. The lower reaches of the loop are piney and open. The vegetation thickens farther up the hollow, allowing more site privacy. The campsites are well established and spacious. Landscaping timbers have been strategically placed where needed.

Loop B forms a figure eight along an arm of Hiwassee Lake. The 15 sites there are located in a grassy glade beneath tall pines. The five most popular campsites in this loop fit snugly against the lake.

Pass a few irritating speed bumps and reach Loop C. It also forms a crude figure eight and is a good distance down the main campground road from the first two loops. Enter an open pine forest with spacious campsites. The back side of the loop runs along a small rhododendron-choked branch. This means a more dense understory.

Loop D is located across the road from Loop C and is situated in some rolling woods. It offers the most densely forested sites, with a thick understory of mountain laurel and small trees. The loop is now used as a picnic area and for overflow camping when all the other sites are taken, which is a shame because it's the most attractive loop.

The 180 miles of picturesque, wooded shoreline of Hiwassee Lake are primarily Forest Service–owned, minimizing development. Bass, bream, and crappie are among the species that provide excellent fishing beneath the highlands. The transparent, green waters will lure you in for a swim on a hot summer day. Boaters can access the lake at the boat ramp at the very end of the main campground road.

Two hiking trails meander from the campground around the peninsula. The Mingus Trail starts across from Loop B and runs through pine-oak woods down to the boat ramp. Return to your campsite on the road. The Ramsey Bluff Trail starts at the back of Loop B and winds along the shore of Hiwassee Lake for 2.2 miles and ends at the back of Loop D.

The nearby town of Murphy is worth more than just a supply run. It is a quintessentially quaint town. Absorb the ambience and make sure to visit the Cherokee County Historical Society Museum. You can see what life was like in the pre-industrial era. You'll find that much of the good from that bygone era is still alive today in this slice of Americana.

To get there, from Murphy take Brown Road (NC 1326) NW for 5 miles. Turn left at campground sign. Hanging Dog will be straight ahead.

KEY INFORMATION

Hanging Dog Campground
201 Woodland Drive
Murphy, NC 28906

Operated by: U.S. Forest Service

Information: (704) 837-5152

Open: May 1 to October 31

Individual sites: 68

Each site has: Tent pad, fire ring, picnic table, lantern post

Site assignment: First come, first served; no reservations

Registration: Self-registration on site

Facilities: Piped water, flush toilets

Parking: At campsites only

Fee: $4 per night

Elevation: 1,600 feet

Restrictions:

Pets—On 6-foot leash only

Fires—In fire rings only

Alcoholic beverages—At campsites only

Vehicles—None

Other—14-day stay limit

NORTH CAROLINA

HORSE COVE CAMPGROUND

Robbinsville, North Carolina

Horse Cove is an unpretentious, small campground adjacent to playful Santeelah Creek. Located primarily along Horse Cove Branch, a tributary of Santeelah Creek, Horse Cove has an unpolished, old-time feel with its minimal facilities. In a way, it is two campgrounds: the lower 6, year-round sites and the upper 11, warm-weather sites. The lower, year-round sites on Santeelah Creek are across Forest Service Road 416 from the main campground. They have a spur road of their own. A pit toilet is the only amenity, although water is available from a spigot in summer and the creek in winter. These sites overlook Santeelah Creek from a heavily wooded knoll.

The upper campground runs up a narrow valley carved by Horse Cove Branch, which forms the western campground border. A steep mountainside hems in the campground to the east, but the campsites are graded and kept level with landscaping timbers. This hillside arrangement spreads campsites apart both horizontally and vertically. A comfort station with low-flow, flush toilets for each sex is located at the campground entrance. You're never far from one of the three water spigots that are conveniently placed about this cozy encampment.

A spare, gravel road divides the upper campground. The five sites beyond Horse Cove Branch are more open and dry beneath

CAMPGROUND RATINGS

Beauty:	★★★★
Site privacy:	★★★★
Site spaciousness:	★★★★★
Quiet:	★★★★
Security:	★★★★
Cleanliness/upkeep:	★★★★

Stay at Horse Cove Campground and see the lovely trees of Joyce Kilmer Memorial Forest and the Slickrock Wilderness.

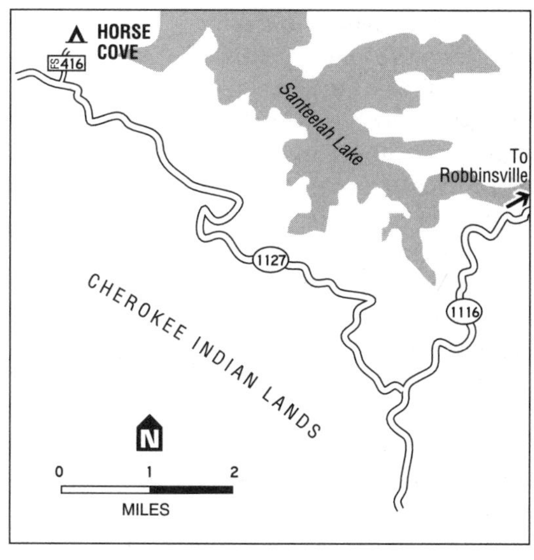

a hardwood canopy. They are well spread along the road, which makes a short loop. The grassy center of the loop has a horseshoe pit. The six campsites adjacent to boisterous Horse Cove Branch are isolated from each other by large rocks intermingled with rhododendron and hemlock. The Horse Cove Trail leads to the high country right from the upper campground, but then ends and splits into two trails along divergent railroad grades remaining from the logging days.

Horse Cove is a nice campground, but the reason for its existence is its proximity to the magnificent Joyce Kilmer Memorial Forest and the adjoining Slickrock Wilderness. Hikers love to walk among the giants of this forest, named for the late writer Joyce Kilmer. He met an untimely end in France during World War I on July 30, 1918. This accomplished author penned a famous poem entitled "Trees." The first two lines of this poem are: "I think that I shall never see/A poem as lovely as a tree."

After his death, a nationwide search ensued to locate a forest grand enough to memorialize Kilmer. Finally, a tract in North Carolina was selected. What we see today is a 3,800-acre, old-growth woodland that is one of the most impressive remnants of what the Southern Appalachians looked like before the loggers permanently altered the landscape.

Several trails start at the Joyce Kilmer Memorial Forest parking area, which is .7 mile west of the Horse Cove Campground on FS 416. The Joyce Kilmer National Recreation Trail forms a figure-eight as it loops through the forest. The .8-mile upper loop that travels through Poplar Cove is said to have the densest concentration of large trees in eastern North America. Tulip trees, twenty feet around the base, rise to meet the sun amidst their fellow forest dwellers: hemlock, beech, and oak. The largest cucumber tree in North Carolina is marked with a plaque. Rhododendron, mountain laurel, and other plants form an understory fighting for the remaining light that filters to the ground.

You can't go wrong with any of the three trails that lead out of Joyce Kilmer Memorial Forest into the high country of the Joyce Kilmer–Slickrock Wilderness. A loop hike of differing combinations is possible using any of the Stratton Bald, Naked Ground, and Jenkins Meadow/ Haoe Lead trails. For a scenic blockbuster of a hike, take the old Cherokee trading path, known to modern hikers as the Naked Ground Trail. It climbs 4.3 miles to Naked Ground, named for its lack of trees in days gone by. To your left, it is 1.3 miles to Bob Stratton Bald, a mile-high mountain meadow with rewarding views of the Smoky and Nantahala forests. The meadow has been restored to its former size by the Forest Service. Since the cessation of cattle grazing, the field had begun to reforest. In the late 1980s, however, trees were cut back and native grasses were planted. Consequently, the meadow and its beautiful views were restored. It's my favorite place in this wilderness.

From Naked Ground, it is 1.4 miles (right) to Hangover Lead. This sheer, rocky drop-off needs no assistance from the Forest Service to maintain its views. The Smoky Mountains and Gregory Bald's open field are visible to your right. The lakes and mountains that are the legacy of western North Carolina and eastern Tennessee are all around you. Return via Naked Ground or Haoe Lead.

KEY INFORMATION

Horse Cove Campground
Route 1, Box 16-A
Robbinsville, NC 28771

Operated by: U.S. Forest Service

Information: (704) 479-6431

Open: Upper campground, April 15 to October 31; lower campground, year-round

Individual sites: 17

Each site has: Tent pad, fire grate, picnic table, lantern post

Site assignment: First come, first served; no reservations

Registration: Self-registration on site

Facilities: Piped water (in summer), flush toilets in summer, vault toilets in winter

Parking: At individual sites

Fee: $5 per night April to October; no fee in winter

Elevation: 2,300 feet

Restrictions:

Pets—On leash only

Fires—In fire grates only

Alcoholic beverages—At campsites only

Vehicles—None

Other—14-day stay limit

To get there, from Robbinsville take U.S. 129 north for 1 mile, then turn left on NC 1116. Go 3.5 miles to NC 1127 and turn right. Go 12 miles to FS 416 and turn right; FS 416 soon bisects the campground.

NORTH CAROLINA

MOUNT MITCHELL STATE PARK

Asheville, North Carolina

Bring warm clothes on your trip to Mount Mitchell. The rarefied air up there more resembles Canada than the South. The flora and fauna follow suit. Luckily, in 1915, then North Carolina Governor Locke Craig recognized the special character of this mountaintop and made it North Carolina's first state park. Now, with a tent-only campground and some superlative highland scenery, Mount Mitchell is a Southern Appalachian highlight.

As the last Ice Age retreated north, cold-weather plants and animals of the north retreated with them—except for those that survived on the highest peaks down in Dixie. These mountaintops formed, in effect, cool-climate islands where the northern species continue to survive. That is what makes Mount Mitchell special. Unfortunately, the mountaintop is under siege by acid rain, insect pests, and a severe climate. As a result, some trees and plants are dying. As you explore Mount Mitchell, try to think of ways we can all help the highland forests.

Mount Mitchell's campground is for tents only, unless you can carry an RV from the parking area up the stone steps to the campground. The short walk immediately enters the dense forest once dominated by the Fraser fir. Today, stunted and weather-beaten mountain ash and a few other hardwoods mingle with the firs.

CAMPGROUND RATINGS

Beauty: ★★★★★
Site privacy: ★★★★
Site spaciousness: ★★★
Quiet: ★★★★
Security: ★★★★★
Cleanliness/upkeep: ★★★★★

Mount Mitchell is the highest point in the eastern United States, and also has the highest tent-only campground at 6,320 feet.

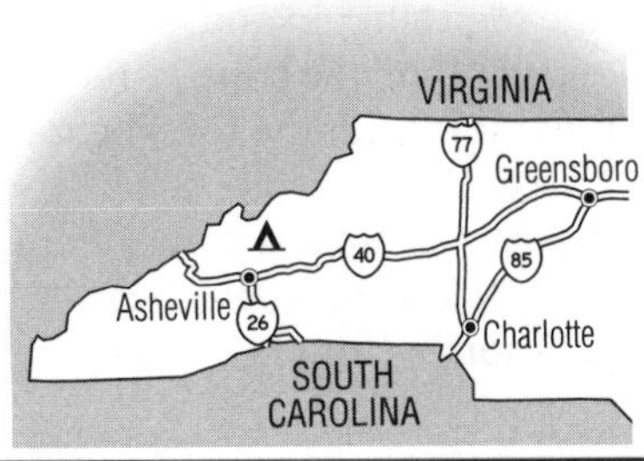

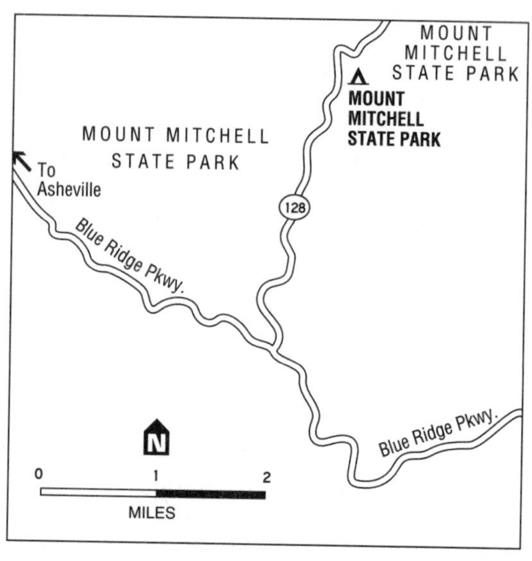

Dead trees remind you of the troubles these forests face.

The nine campsites splinter off the gravel path that rises with the mountainside. They are set into the land amid the dense woods. The sites are small and fairly close together, but are private due to the heavy plant growth. There is little canopy overhead, as the trees become gnarled the higher they grow. There are two water spigots along the short path. A bathroom with flush toilets for each sex is midway along the path. Firewood is for sale at $3 per bundle in the parking area.

Sites 1 and 9 are the most private, but feel lucky to get a site at all during summer weekends. With only nine sites, this tiny campground exudes an intimate, secluded feel. The only noise you'll hear is the wind whipping over your head. By the way, Mount Mitchell is covered in fog, rain, or snow eight out of ten days per year. Snow has been recorded every month of the year. Annually it receives 104 inches of snow. Don't let those facts deter you; weather is part of the phenomenon that is Mount Mitchell.

The fog rolled in and out of the campground during our mid-summer trip. Now and then the sun would shine, warming us. Wooded ridges came in and out of view with the fog; the whole scene seemed like some other world.

Carry a jacket along when you tramp the park. First drive up to the summit parking area and make the short jaunt to the observation tower atop Mount Mitchell. There lies the remains of Elisha Mitchell, who fell to his death from a cliff after measuring the height of the mountain. From the tower you can see the Black Mountain Range and beyond. Back near the parking area, check out the museum that details the natural history of Mount Mitchell.

Many hiking trails thread the park. From the campground you can walk to the observation tower and connect to the Deep Gap Trail; it's a rugged 6-mile hike along the Black Mountain Range to several peaks that stand over 6,000 feet in elevation. Or you can leave the campground on the Old Mount Mitchell Trail past the park restaurant and loop around Mount Hallback to return to the campground.

Mount Mitchell State Park is surrounded by the Pisgah National Forest and the Blue Ridge Parkway. This, in essence, increases the forest area of the 1,677-acre state park. Many national forest trails connect to the state park trails, allowing nearly unlimited hiking opportunities. Procure a trail map from the park office for the best hiking experience.

Get your supplies in Asheville before you leave. The Blue Ridge Parkway makes for a scenic drive, but once in the highlands of the Black Mountains, you won't want to leave this wonderful mountaintop and campground.

To get there, from Asheville take the Blue Ridge Parkway north for 34 miles to milepost 355. Turn left into Mount Mitchell State Park. The campground is 4 miles up the road on your right.

KEY INFORMATION

Mount Mitchell State Park
Route 5, Box 700
Burnsville, NC 28714

Operated by: North Carolina State Parks

Information: (704) 675-4611

Open: May 1 to October 31

Individual sites: 9

Each site has: Tent pad, grill, picnic table

Site assignment: First come, first served; no reservations

Registration: Ranger will come by and register you

Facilities: Piped water, flush toilets, pay phone

Parking: At tent campers' parking area only

Fee: $9 per night

Elevation: 6,320 feet

Restrictions:

Pets—On 6-foot leash only

Fires—In fire grates only

Alcoholic beverages—Prohibited

Vehicles—None

Other—No gathering firewood in the park

NELSON'S NANTAHALA HIDEAWAY CAMPGROUND

Andrews, North Carolina

The owners of this campground knew they had a good location for tent campers to access the numerous outdoor features in the immediate vicinity, so they set about creating a quality campground to match the first-rate scenery of the area. They're still working out a few kinks, but you will be more than satisfied with your stay here.

Pass the campground office, which has ice and soft-drink machines, and enter the campground. The campground design features the classic loop, which climbs up the side of a hill along a small creek, Powder Burnt Branch. The campsites are set along tiers that extend from one side of the loop to the other. Because of the tiers, campers enjoy topographic relief yet don't have to camp on a slope, as the tiers are level and evenly graded.

Several generations ago the campground was a cornfield. Later, trees reclaimed the site. When the campground was built, the quality trees were left to flourish. Now, Nelson's Hideaway has been well landscaped. The lower end of the loop is more open. Tree cover thickens as the campground rises. A thick carpet of grass forms the campground understory.

Water spigots are spread throughout the campground. The centrally located bathhouse is simply the finest I've ever seen this side of a fancy hotel, much less a campground. Divided by sex, each attractive

CAMPGROUND RATINGS

Beauty:	★★★
Site privacy:	★★★
Site spaciousness:	★★★★
Quiet:	★★★★
Security:	★★★★
Cleanliness/upkeep:	★★★★★

This new campground may be hidden, but it offers easy access to the Nantahala River Gorge and numerous biking and hiking trails.

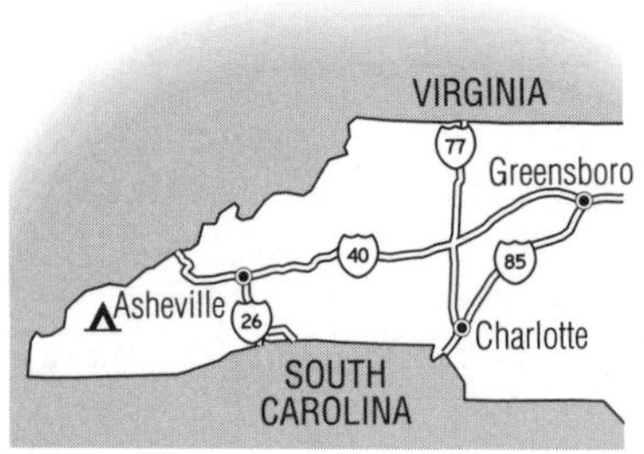

section contains three hot showers and flush toilets inside the rustic, wood exterior. Wash your dirty duds in the laundry, which is located here as well.

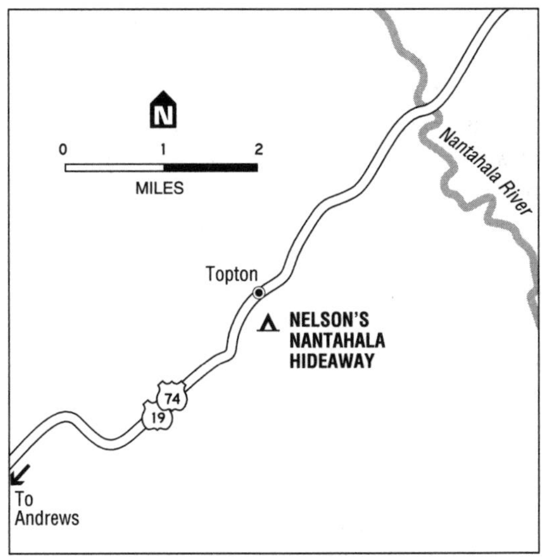

If you don't feel like pitching your tent, use one of the Adirondack-style, open-air shelters at the beginning of the loop. They have padded bunks and a small porch to enjoy the cool mountain breezes. The shelters have a picnic table beside them, too. Three sizable group campsites are located in a flat across Powder Burnt Branch. They can be reached by crossing a small footbridge.

The woods thicken at the top of the loop. This area is most popular with tent campers. You are the king of the hill. There, campers can see across the valley to the Snowbird Mountains.

The middle tiers of the campground are equipped with electricity in addition to the regular amenities. But don't expect too many RVs here. It's a steep climb to the campground from the highway. In addition, active campers are more likely to be found here, with all the hiking, canoeing, and kayaking opportunities.

Just 2 miles north is the Nantahala River Launch Site. There, canoers and kayakers enter the river gorge for a 9-mile run of nationally known whitewater floating. Commercial outfitters will accommodate inexperienced thrill-seekers who long to challenge the chilly, continuous rapids.

The Nelson family has built hiking trails on its land that connect to the Apple Tree national forest trails that border the campground. This is only fitting, since earlier family generations actually sold the Apple Tree land to the federal government to form a section of the Nantahala National Forest. These forest trails follow old Cherokee routes that connected their lands in western Carolina and eastern Tennessee.

The London Bald Trail is closest to the campground property. It is reached from Piercy Creek. The London Bald Trail in turn connects to Laurel Creek and Diamond Valley trails for numerous loop-hiking opportunities. The Bartram National Scenic Trail can be easily reached via the London Bald Trail. Consult the campground office for a hiking map.

Adjacent to the campground is a cool, clear fishing pond. An old-fashioned waterwheel oxygenates the water, where trout thrive. For stream fishing, head to nearby Piercy Creek. Nantahala Lake is just a few miles east for lake-fishing possibilities. An assortment of mountain biking trails threads the national forestland nearby, which nearly envelopes the campground.

Combine the fine, new facilities of Nelson's Nantahala Hideaway with the recreational variety of this section of western North Carolina and you have a successful tent-camping adventure.

To get there, from Andrews take U.S. 19/74 north for 6 miles to the community of Topton. Nelson's Nantahala Hideaway will be on your right.

KEY INFORMATION

Nelson's Nantahala Hideaway Campground
P.O. Box 25, U.S. 19/74
Topton, NC 28781

Operated by: Jimmy Kyle Davis

Information: (704) 321-4407

Open: April 15 to October 31

Individual sites: 30

Each site has: Tent area, picnic table, fire ring

Site assignment: First come, first served or by reservation

Registration: At campground office

Facilities: Hot showers, piped water, laundry, soft-drink machine, some electrical hookups

Parking: At campsites only

Fee: $12 per night for 2 people; $2 each additional person

Elevation: 2,800 feet

Restrictions:

Pets—On leash only

Fires—In fire rings only

Alcoholic beverages—At campsites only

Vehicles—None

NORTH CAROLINA

NORTH MILLS RIVER CAMPGROUND

Asheville, North Carolina

North Mills River Campground lies on the very edge of the Pisgah National Forest. But you would never know it by the sylvan setting of the area, divided by the free-flowing North Mills River, which has cut a valley amid the Carolina mountains. All roads leading to and within the campground are paved, which lures in a few extra RVers. Overall, this is an unhurried, family-atmosphere campground that is rarely filled to capacity.

As you approach the campground, it seems much larger than it really is, due to the sizable picnic area adjacent to the campground. To your right is a half-moon-shaped camping loop containing 13 campsites. These sites are in a very level area lying between the North Mills River and a steep hill. Tall shade trees grow high over the grassy understory. The five sites inside the half-moon are spread far apart and are very open. These sites are for the campers with excess gear who don't mind a slight sacrifice in privacy. Some sites on the outside of the loop are set into the hillside and are less level. The campground host resides on this loop. Four water spigots are evenly spaced among the campsites. A comfort station with flush toilets for each sex is at the loop's center.

Over a bridge across the North Mills River is the main campground loop. These 19 sites are on a slight slope declining toward the river. As you drive along the

CAMPGROUND RATINGS

Beauty:	★★★
Site privacy:	★★★★
Site spaciousness:	★★★★
Quiet:	★★★★
Security:	★★★★
Cleanliness/upkeep:	★★★★

North Mills River Campground offers a worthy sampling of the southern Blue Ridge country.

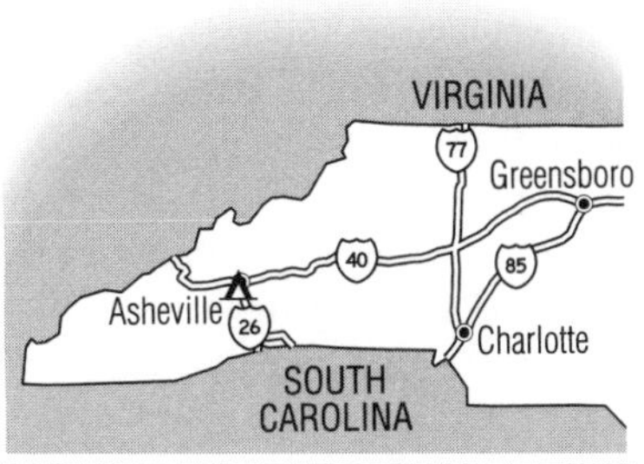

one-way road, a field appears on the inside of the loop. Four spacious and open sites are set in the field. One of these is a double site for groups. A short spur road dead-ends off this loop and leads to three smaller campsites; this trio offers the most isolation in the entire campground.

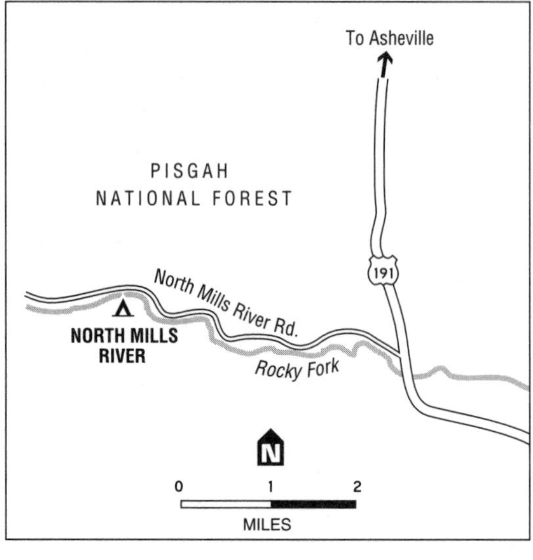

As you continue along the main loop, the field ends and a hemlock, fern, and rhododendron understory begins among nearly hidden campsites. This understory is very thick, especially as the loop parallels the river. Three single sites and one double site are located riverside beneath tall evergreens. Four water spigots are situated along the loop. A lighted bathroom lies in the dark and forested center of the loop.

North Mills River is used mostly by local families. Children float down the river in inner tubes, and anglers fish for trout, while others explore the nearby forest trails. As summer evenings darken and cool down, campers often meander from site to site and get to know their neighbors. Don't be surprised if you are paid a friendly visit and offered a cup of coffee by your fellow camper. The campground host is often the center of these social gatherings.

To get a good lay of the land combined with a little history, take a scenic forest drive. Gravel Forest Service Road 1206 leaves the campground just beyond the self-service pay station. It will lead you to the Pink Beds Visitor Center. The Pink Beds is a 6,800-acre mountain valley where professional forestry was first practiced in the United States. It is a National Historic Site complete with a museum that tells of the evolution of forestry in our country. Two interpretive trails enhance the story of George Vanderbilt's management of his forestland. This valley is also known as the Cradle of Forestry in America.

To complete your scenic drive, turn right on U.S. 276 from the Pink Beds and intersect the Blue Ridge Parkway after 3.8 miles. The Blue Ridge Parkway extends for 469 miles, linking the Great Smoky Mountains and Shenandoah national parks. Head north on the parkway and enjoy some of the scenery for which this road is known. Stop and climb the 1-mile Frying Pan Mountain Trail to the lookout tower at its peak. Farther north is your right turn back onto gravel FS 479 and back down to the Mills River Recreation Area.

Informal hiking and fishing trails fan out from the campground. Several marked trails start 2 miles from the campground up FS 479 just after its junction with FS 142. The Big Creek Trail (#102) and Trace Ridge Trail (#354) are two trails of note. They both leave the North Mills River watershed to intersect the Blue Ridge Parkway and the high country. If you're not sure exactly where to go, just ask your neighbor. Most local folks in the campground will gladly steer you onto a nearby good path. After all, they're quite proud of their mountain lands.

To get there, from Asheville follow NC 191 south for 13.3 miles to North Mills River Road (NC 1345). Turn right at the campground sign and follow North Mills River Road for 5 miles, intersecting the North Mills River Campground.

KEY INFORMATION

North Mills River Campground
P.O. Box 8
Pisgah Forest, NC 28768

Operated by: U.S. Forest Service

Information: (704) 877-3265

Open: Entire campground, March 15 to October 31; 13 sites, year-round

Individual sites: 32

Each site has: Tent pad, fire grate, lantern post, picnic table

Site assignment: First come, first served; no reservations

Registration: Self-registration on site

Facilities: Flush toilets, piped water in spring, summer, and fall; no water, chemical toilets in winter

Parking: At campsites only

Fee: $6 per night

Elevation: 2,500 feet

Restrictions:

Pets—On leash only

Fires—In fire grates only

Alcoholic beverages—At campsites only

Vehicles—None

Other—14-day stay limit

PRICE PARK CAMPGROUND

Boone, North Carolina

Located high in the forests of the Blue Ridge Mountains, Price Park has a quality campground and plenty of activities that don't involve an automobile. Don't let the size of the campground scare you off. There are a lot of sites; however, one area is for RV-camping only and another area is for one-night campers only. Yet another area allows both RV and tent camping.

The one-night-only camping loop is backed against the shores of Price Lake. The south end of the paved loop is thickly forested, both overhead and on the ground for maximum privacy. Five of the sites are right along the lakeshore. The other end of the loop circles a field and is more open. A few pull-through RV sites are here. A lighted bathroom is conveniently placed at the center of the loop for all campers to share. Two water spigots are located at each end of this spacious and private loop.

The main RV/tent area has three loops. Loops C and D spur off the larger Loop B. Oddly enough, Loop D is actually inside Loop B. Loop C spurs off on its own. They are all in a rolling woodland and tastefully set into the mountains without dominating the natural landscape. The plethora of trees overhead reminds you that you are in the forest. The rhododendron understory provides enough privacy; however, it isn't everywhere, which allows you to move about the campground freely.

CAMPGROUND RATINGS

Beauty:	★★★★★
Site privacy:	★★★
Site spaciousness:	★★★★
Quiet:	★★★★
Security:	★★★★
Cleanliness/upkeep:	★★★★★

This campground is part of the Blue Ridge Parkway, yet it offers more than just a stopping place between scenic drives.

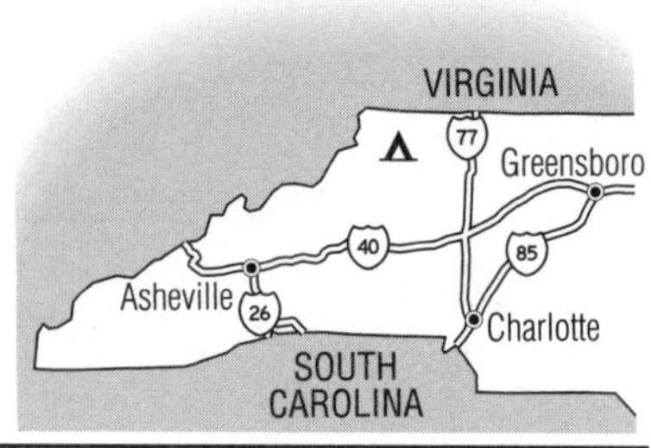

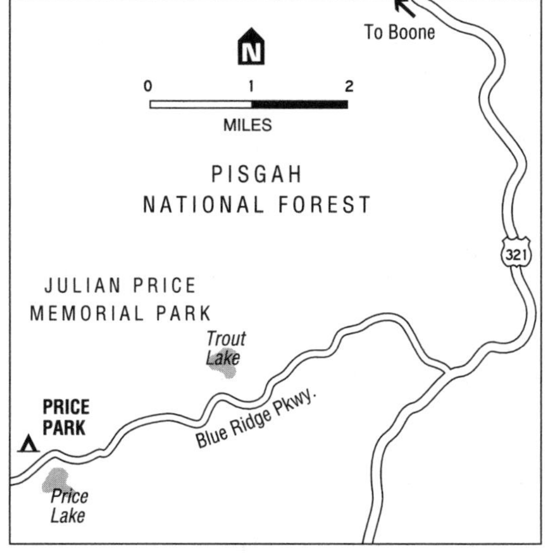

Landscaping timbers were used where site leveling was necessary. Some of the sites in Loops B and C are a tad close together, but with investigating and luck, you can find a private site. There are nine water spigots spread throughout these three loops for easy water access. The three lighted bathrooms ensure you never have to go too far if nature calls in the middle of the night.

Loops E and F are for RVs only and concentrate these campers in one location. On my visit to Price Park, I didn't see any other RVers outside the RV-only loops, with the exception of a couple in the one-night-only loop. Expect a full house on hot summer weekends when nearby lowlanders escape the heat. A ranger and a campground host reside at the campground to answer questions and ease your safety concerns.

Even the most ardent auto tourists have to stretch their legs every once in a while and see for themselves just what is beyond the roadside. Price Park offers the Blue Ridge sightseer plenty to do outside the car. Trails actually run through the campground, which makes starting a hike even easier.

The Boone Fork Trail makes a 5-mile loop passing through many environments of the Blue Ridge. It leaves the campground to enter a meadow and picks up an old farm road. It then runs along Bee Tree Creek, crossing it 16 times. Pass through a rocky area and return to the campground through a meadow.

The 2.3-mile Green Knob Trail climbs to an overlook that will reward you with well-earned views of Price Lake, then loops back via Sims Pond. The

Tanawha Trail runs for 13 miles south along the Blue Ridge Parkway and obviously requires a shuttle. A segment of the North Carolina Mountains-to-Sea Trail passes through Price Park on its proposed way to the ocean.

The Price Lake Trail makes a 2.3-mile loop around the 47-acre Price Lake. The lake contains three species of trout for you to try to catch: rainbow, brook, and brown. Nearby Sims Pond has only the native brook trout. Stream fishermen can try Boone Fork and Sims Creek for trout as well. A valid North Carolina fishing license is required.

During the 1940s, Julian Price bought this area as a retreat for his company employees. His heirs willed the area to the park service for all of us to enjoy. As scenic as the Blue Ridge Parkway is, you may find this special area hard to pass by. Stop and spend a day enjoying the Blue Ridge with no glass between you and nature.

To get there, from Boone take U.S. 321 east for 7 miles to the Blue Ridge Parkway. Turn south on the parkway and follow it for 7 miles to Julian Price Memorial Park. The campground check-in station will be on your right.

KEY INFORMATION

Price Park Campground
200 BB & T Building,
One Pack Square
Asheville, NC 28801

Operated by: National Park Service

Information: (704) 298-0398

Open: May 1 to October 31

Individual sites: 129

Each site has: Tent pad, picnic table, fire grate, lantern post

Site assignment: First come, first served; no reservations

Registration: Register at campground check-in station

Facilities: Flush toilets, piped water, pay phone

Parking: At campsites only

Fee: $10 per night for 2 people; $2 each additional person over 18

Elevation: 3,400 feet

Restrictions:

Pets—On a 6-foot leash only

Fires—In fire grates only

Alcoholic beverages—At campsites only

Vehicles—30-foot trailer length limit

Other—14-day stay limit; 30-day total limit for calendar year

ROCKY BLUFF CAMPGROUND

Hot Springs, North Carolina

CAMPGROUND RATINGS

Beauty:	★★★★★
Site privacy:	★★★
Site spaciousness:	★★★
Quiet:	★★★★
Security:	★★★★
Cleanliness/upkeep:	★★★★

The design of this campground will capture your fancy and the setting will make you stay.

As I headed down into the Rocky Bluff Recreation Area, I found it hard to believe there was a campground down there. The road dipped into very hilly terrain, with nary a flat spot to be found. But soon enough there was the beginning of Rocky Bluff Campground. With the price of today's manpower, this campground would simply not have been built.

"Engineering marvel" may be a stretch, but a ton or two of site leveling and stone work had to be done to tastefully fit this campground into the wooded dips and rises of the land. All the stone work makes your back ache just looking at it.

Rocky Bluff Campground is divided into two loops. Enter the lower loop as you pass the pay station. Three shaded sites are dug into the hillside and reinforced with the above-mentioned stonework. Five open sites sit on the inside of the loop and are on what passes for flat ground here at Rocky Bluff.

At the low point of the lower loop, a road spurs off to the right and leads to the upper loop. As the road makes a steep climb, two campsites are somehow fit into the terrain. Seven sites lie on top of the hill, spread along the road as it makes a short loop to return to the main campground. Two sites feature a view into Spring Creek hollow to the east.

A warning to those who get spooked easily: Also atop this hill, right next to the

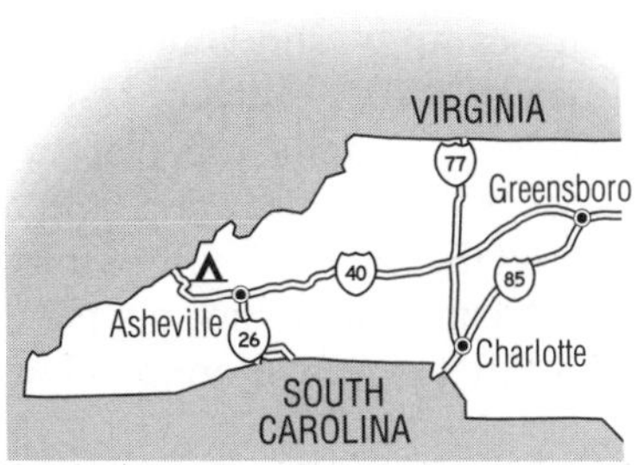

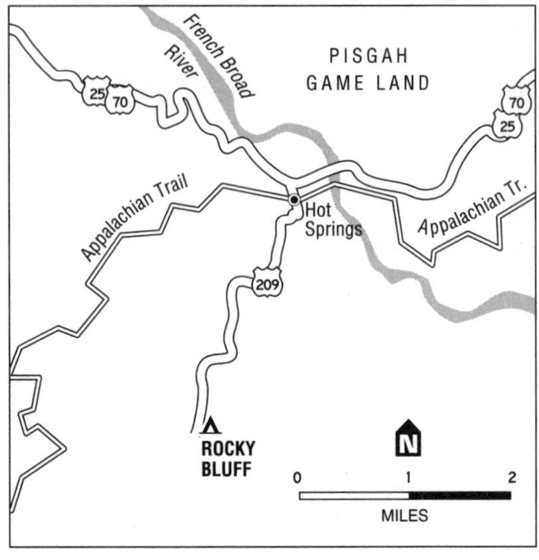

campsites, is the Brooks Cemetery. Three sites have a view of the cemetery. Stay down on the lower loop if the proximity of the cemetery will prevent you from getting a sound night's sleep.

Intersect the lower loop again from the upper loop road. There, sites are strewn in the open, lightly wooded center of the loop; a few others are tucked away in the thickets outside the loop. There isn't a whole lot of privacy. Due to the sloping terrain, you are probably going to be looking down on another camper or vice versa. And a generally grassy understory doesn't shield you much from your neighbor, either. The upper loop is more wooded, where ironically you might want to keep your neighbor in view to make sure he isn't a ghost roaming from the cemetery.

The lower loop road passes a picnic area on the right and returns to the pay station. This loop has the only comfort station for the 30-site campground. Those on the upper loop must walk down the hill to use the facilities. But water spigots are conveniently placed around both loops for your convenience.

This campground is neat. The terrain and stonework make it unique. The cemetery adds a touch of history and mystique. If the cemetery isn't enough of the past, imagine this place a century ago when there was a community of homes, a blacksmith shop, and even a school!

Now the nearest community is Hot Springs. It embodies small town Appalachia, full of nice people who work hard for a living in the splendor of a land that is now more precious to them than ever before. The Appalachian

Trail runs right through town. Visit the Pisgah National Forest Visitor Center. And you've got to check out the hot springs for which the community was named.

Outdoor pastimes are plentiful. Several outfitters in town will arrange a white-water rafting trip down the French Broad, which flows through Hot Springs. A 6-mile biking trail runs along the river to Paint Rock, which marks the Tennessee–North Carolina state line. This dividing line starts across the bridge over the French Broad from Hot Springs. The AT crosses this bridge, too. Hike either way on the AT until your legs wear out.

Two fulfilling trails depart from Rocky Bluff Campground. The 1.2-mile Spring Creek Nature Trail loops down to Spring Creek and follows it a good ways before veering north and intersecting the campground again. This is a rewarding and short day hike. The Van Cliff Loop Trail is a little longer and tougher. It leaves the campground and climbs, crossing NC 209 on the way. It hooks up into some piney woods before returning to the welcome campground after 2.6 miles.

To get there, from Hot Springs take NC 209 south for 3 miles. Rocky Bluff Campground will be on your left.

KEY INFORMATION

Rocky Bluff Campground
P.O. Box 128
Hot Springs, NC 28743

Operated by: U.S. Forest Service

Information: (704) 622-3202

Open: May 1 to October 31

Individual sites: 30

Each site has: Tent pad, fire grate, lantern post, picnic table

Site assignment: First come, first served; no reservations

Registration: Self-registration on site

Facilities: Flush toilets, piped water

Parking: At campsites only

Fee: $5 per night

Elevation: 1,780 feet

Restrictions:

Pets—On a 6-foot leash only

Fires—In fire grates only

Alcoholic beverages—At campsites only

Vehicles—18-foot trailer length limit

Other—14-day stay limit

STANDING INDIAN CAMPGROUND

Franklin, North Carolina

According to Cherokee legend, a warrior was once posted on top of a certain mountain to look out for a flying monster that had swept away a child from a nearby village. The villagers prayed to the Great Spirit to annihilate the monster. A violent storm struck the mountain reducing it to rock, turning the lookout warrior into a stone "Standing Indian."

The Nantahala River is born on Standing Indian Mountain just upstream from this outstanding, high-country campground, where cool breezes from the ridgetops temper the warm summer air. With sites on five loops, the campground is spread out and offers the camper varying site conditions. The first loop diffuses along the Nantahala with hemlock-shaded sites isolated by thick stands of rhododendron. Across the river, three loops are spread out in a large, flat area interspersed with large hardwoods that allow plenty of sun and grass to flourish among their ranks. Ritter Lumber Company once had a logging camp here. Farther back still, across Kimsey Creek, are mountainside sites. They stand level, among the sloping forest of yellow birch, beech, and sugar maple, separated by lush greenery that makes each site seem isolated. Six double sites accommodate larger groups.

Campground hosts occupy each loop for your safety and convenience. Sixteen water pumps are strategically located

CAMPGROUND RATINGS

Beauty:	★★★★★
Site privacy:	★★★★
Site spaciousness:	★★★★★
Quiet:	★★★
Security:	★★★★
Cleanliness/upkeep:	★★★★

Soak in the mountains of the Standing Indian Basin from the headwaters of the Nantahala River.

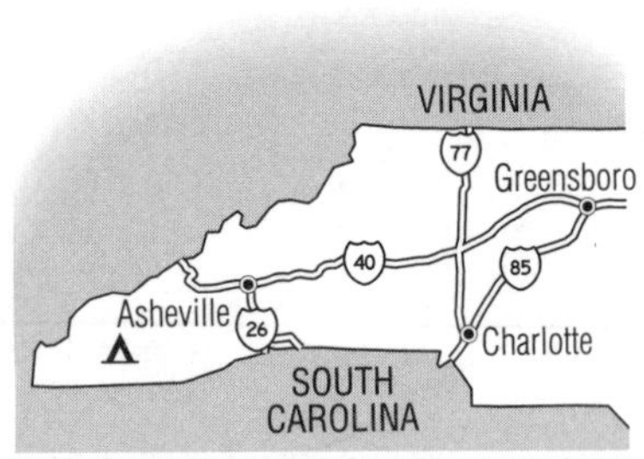

throughout the loops, in addition to five comfort stations with flush toilets. Two of the comfort stations have hot showers. You may pick up dead, downed firewood from the surrounding area without a permit. Keep in mind that Standing Indian can be crowded during peak summer weekends.

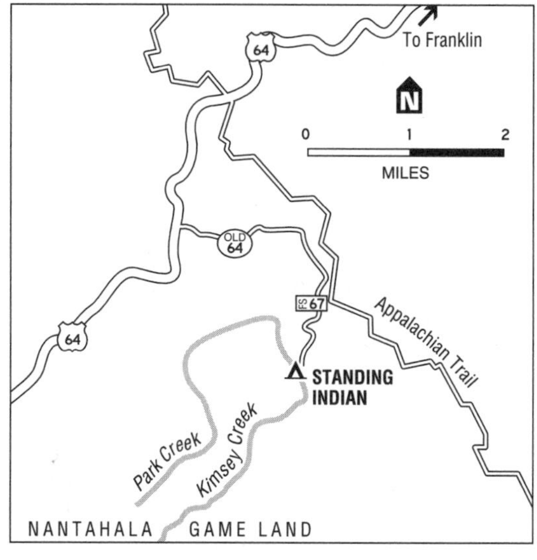

There's plenty to do nearby. Try your luck at one of the campground horseshoe pits. Fish for trout on the Nantahala River or Kimsey Creek. Rainbow and brown trout are the predominant cold-water fish in the streams, with some brook trout in the upper waters. For the nonfishing water lover, there are two falls nearby. Drive 5 miles on Forest Service Road 67 beyond the turnoff to the campground. The Big Laurel Falls Trail sign is on the right. After passing over a footbridge, the trail splits. Veer to the right and come to Big Laurel Falls in .5 mile. The Mooney Falls Trail starts .7 mile beyond the Big Laurel Falls trailhead and leads .1 mile to the cascading falls.

Several trails begin at the campground itself. To orient yourself, find the Backcountry Information Center located .2 mile left of the campground entrance gate. Study the map. Make an 8-mile loop out of the Park Creek and Park Ridge trails. The Park Creek Trail starts at the Backcountry Information Center. Follow it down the Nantahala then up Park Creek to Park Gap. Take the Park Ridge Trail 3.2 miles back down to the campground. This hike is rated moderate to strenuous, with a net elevation change of 880 feet.

The most prominent trail in the area is the famed Appalachian Trail, which skirts the campground to the south and east. This 87-mile section from the

Georgia line to the Smokies is considered by many hikers to be one of the most rugged sections, with its relentlessly steep ups and downs. This section weeds out many Appalachian Trail thru-hikers who aspire to "follow the white blaze" 2,100 miles to Maine.

The AT passes by FS 67 on the way to the campground. Drive out of the campground toward Wallace Gap about a mile. The Rock Gap parking area is on your right. Take the AT south (uphill to your right) and soon you'll come to the Rock Gap backcountry shelter. These shelters are located about one day's walk from one another along the entire AT. They provide a haven from the elements for the weary thru-hiker. Imagine this as your home for a six-month journey up the spine of the Appalachians.

While you're at Standing Indian Campground, why not see the mountain it was named for? It's a strenuous 3.9-mile climb to the 5,499-foot peak, but the views provide ample reward. Use the Lower Ridge Trail, which starts on the left just beyond the campground bridge over the Nantahala. Switchback up to the ridgecrest and follow it southward to the Appalachian Trail. Take a spur trail .2 mile to the top of Standing Indian. View the Blue Ridge Mountains and the Tallulah River Basin.

To get there, from Franklin drive west on U.S. 64 for 9 miles to old U.S. 64. Following the sign to Standing Indian, turn left and go 1.5 miles to Wallace Gap. Turn right at the sign on FS 67 leading to the campground.

KEY INFORMATION

Standing Indian Campground
90 Sloan Road
Franklin, NC 28734

Operated by: MJK Enterprises

Information: (704) 524-6441

Open: April 1 to December 15

Individual sites: 84

Each site has: Tent pad, fire grate, lantern post, picnic table

Site assignment: First come, first served

Registration: Self-registration on site

Facilities: Drinking water, flush toilets, hot showers, public phone

Parking: At campsites only

Fee: $10 per night

Elevation: 3,400 feet

Restrictions:

Pets—On a leash only

Fires—In fire grates only

Alcoholic beverages—At campsites only

Vehicles—21-foot trailer length limit

Other—Sites limited to 1 family or 5 persons

STONE MOUNTAIN STATE PARK

Elkin, North Carolina

Perched on the eastern edge of the Blue Ridge Mountains, Stone Mountain State Park is a 13,000-acre preserve of granite domes and hardwoods, where wild trout streams and hiking trails thread the land. Stone Mountain Campground, quiet and punctuated with just the right amenities, merely clinches the decision to visit here.

Stone Mountain Campground is situated in a mixed hardwood forest adjacent to a grassy meadow. Two loops provide Stone Mountain tent campers, who compose 90% of the campground users, with a variety of campsite settings.

The first campground loop lies in the shade of moderately sloping woodland. The 13 sites are carved out of a second-growth forest that provides optimum privacy due to the thick stands of young, straight trees racing skyward to the light. The dense growth limits campsite spaciousness, yet offers adequate room for all but the biggest gearheads.

Five of the sites are on the loop's interior, making them closest to the modern comfort station. It includes hot showers, flush toilets for each sex, drinking water, and laundry tubs for those dirty clothes. Piped water is just a few steps away no matter where you are on this loop.

Six more sites abut the open field along the main campground road. Bushes are planted here and there for a little privacy,

CAMPGROUND RATINGS

Beauty:	★★★
Site privacy:	★★★★
Site spaciousness:	★★★★
Quiet:	★★★★
Security:	★★★★★
Cleanliness/upkeep:	★★★★★

The 13,000-acre Stone Mountain State Park is a designated National Natural Landmark.

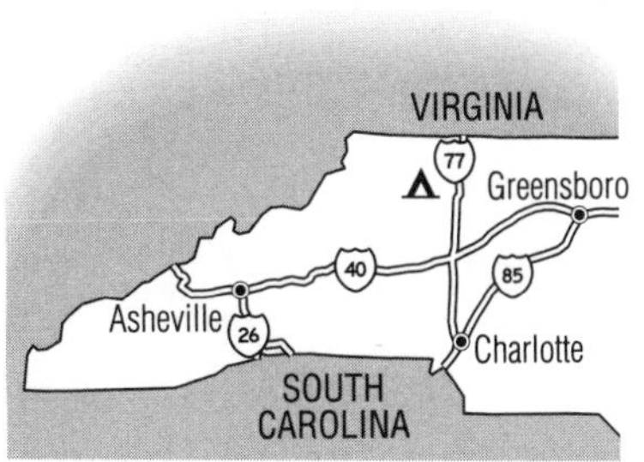

but these sites are still very open. Maximum site spaciousness offsets the lack of privacy. Tent campers who like plenty of sunshine will enjoy these sites.

Farther along the road is a mix of forest and field. The campground host cabin sits there, amid wooded sites on one side of the paved road. The other side of the road features a continuation of the open sites. The road makes a small loop, containing five campsites that are the most private in the entire campground. Piped water is nearby back there, but you must walk to the first loop to access the campground's only comfort station.

A campground host and active, friendly rangers make this a safe and fun place. Park gates open at 8 A.M. and close as the sun sets. This campground fills up on summer weekends. It stands to reason, with all that is going on here at Stone Mountain. Rangers hold interpretive programs for campers to learn about this area's natural and cultural riches.

The granite dome of Stone Mountain is the centerpiece of this park. View the dome from the park office. Rock climbers can be seen scaling the sheer face. If you should engage in this challenging endeavor, register at the park office and the local hospital. A marked hiking trail will lead you to the top of the dome safely.

The trails around Stone Mountain, with the exception of Widows Creek Trail, are all interconnected, making a variety of loops possible. Start at the main trail parking area at the base of Stone Mountain. It is a short but steep .6 mile to the summit of the dome on the Stone Mountain Trail. Westward is the crest of the Blue Ridge. If you continue on, you'll encounter Hitching Rock. There, other prominent park features, Wolf Rock and Cedar Rock, can be seen. Next, pass the 200-foot Stone Mountain Falls on Big Sandy Creek. Complete your loop at 3.3 miles.

Cedar Rock and Wolf Rock trails are rewarding hikes and allow good views of Stone Mountain. The self-guided Nature Trail will familiarize you with the flora of the area. The Widows Creek Trail leads into the isolated northwestern section of the park, where backcountry campers stay overnight.

Trout fishing is a popular pursuit here. Rainbow, brown, and brook trout are all represented in the 17 miles of mountain streams. These waters are accessible along roads and foot trails. Check with the park office, as the creeks have varying fishing regulations.

Stone Mountain has been in the works for millions of years. Man has made his mark only relatively recently. Several historic park structures stand testimony to this fact. Luckily for us, the citizens of North Carolina worked hard to make this a fairly recent inclusion into the state park system. After all this time in development, Stone Mountain is worth more than a few days of your time.

To get there, from Elkin drive north on U.S. 21 for 13 miles to Traphill Road (SR 1002). There will be a sign for the park. Turn left on Traphill Road, following it for 4.3 miles to John P. Frank Parkway. Turn right at the parkway and follow it for 2.5 miles to the park entrance.

KEY INFORMATION

Stone Mountain State Park
Star Route 1, Box 17
Roaring Gap, NC 28668

Operated by: North Carolina State Parks

Information: (910) 957-8185

Open: Year-round

Individual sites: 37

Each site has: Tent pad, fire grate, picnic table

Site assignment: First come, first served; no reservations

Registration: Campground host will come around and register campers

Facilities: Hot showers, flush toilets, piped water

Parking: At campsites only

Fee: $9 per night

Elevation: 2,000 feet

Restrictions:

Pets—On 6-foot leash only

Fires—In fire grates only

Alcoholic beverages—Prohibited

Vehicles—None

Other—14-day stay limit

TSALI CAMPGROUND

Bryson City, North Carolina

What do a Cherokee Indian, a pioneer, a big dam, and mountain biking have in common? Answer: They all played a part in the evolution of Tsali Recreation Area.

Back during the Trail of Tears, a Cherokee leader by the name of Tsali turned himself in so other Cherokee could remain in the area. These Indians formed the nucleus of the Eastern Band of Cherokee who now live on the reservation adjacent to Bryson City. Early in this century, pioneer Harv Brown raised corn along Mouse Branch; there he turned his corn into "corn juice," otherwise known as moonshine. In the 1940s, Fontana Dam was built; Harv and his kinfolk moved away. Now Harv's plot is Tsali Campground, where hikers, horseback riders, and especially mountain bikers congregate. These hearty adventurers catch their collective breath here at Tsali between excursions along the 39 miles of trails that emanate from the campground bordering Fontana Lake.

Tsali Campground is divided into two loops. The upper loop has 22 sites. Plenty of second-growth hardwoods and pines shade the former field. The Forest Service keeps the campground well groomed. A sparse understory makes the campground more open, yet sacrifices privacy. Six of the sites are spread along Mouse Branch. Four water spigots are evenly dispersed

CAMPGROUND RATINGS

Beauty:	★★★★
Site privacy:	★★★
Site spaciousness:	★★★
Quiet:	★★
Security:	★★★★★
Cleanliness/upkeep:	★★★★★

Head straight from the tent and go mountain biking, boating, horseback riding, hiking, and fishing at Tsali Campground.

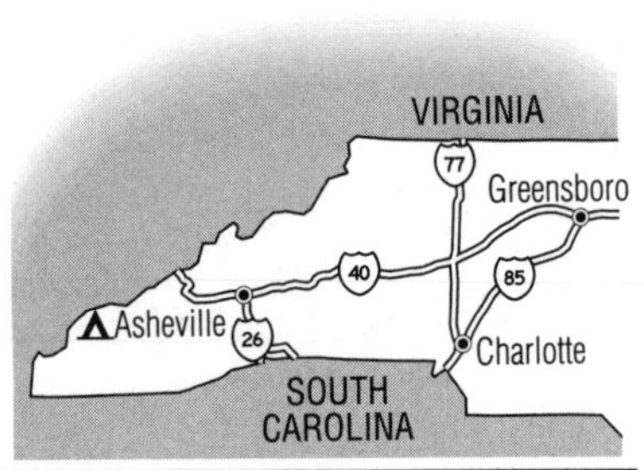

along the loop. A pair of low-volume flush toilets sit in the loop's center.

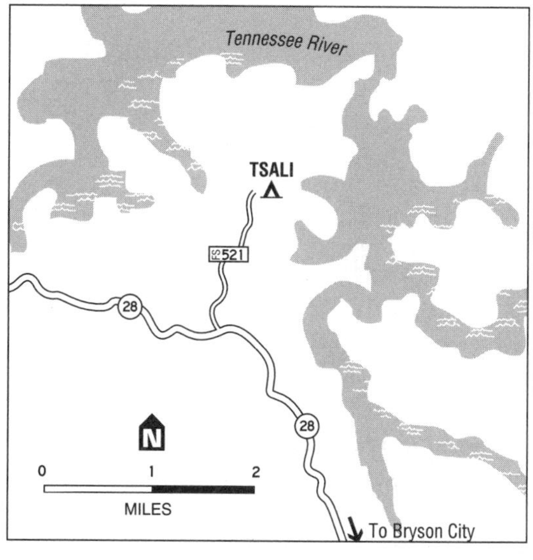

The lower loop features 19 sites and is more open and spacious than the upper loop, having fewer trees and, in certain places, a grassy understory. Eight sites back against Mouse Branch. At the head of the lower loop is a modern rest room facility with flush toilets and hot showers, which are very popular with sweaty hikers and bikers. There are three water spigots near at hand for lower-loop campers. A short trail leads from the lower loop to Fontana Lake.

The campground is full on weekends and busy during the week with active campers. Mountain bikers from all over the Southeast converge on Tsali to ride its trails. Many campers bring canoes as well, to drift on Fontana Lake and glide on the nearby white-water rivers. Hikers abound. Pleasure boaters and equestrians have their fair representation, too.

There are four primary Tsali trails. The Forest Service has devised a workable system for all three groups—hikers, bikers, and equestrians—to enjoy without bothering one another. Hikers can use all four trails at any time. The Right Loop and Left Loop trails are paired together. The Mouse Branch and Thompson Loop trails are paired together in a system whereby equestrians and bikers alternate daily use of the paired trails. The Right Loop Trail is a single-track trail that extends for 11 miles with views of Fontana Lake. It can be shortened to 4-or 8-mile loops. The Left Loop Trail is a 12-mile single-track pathway that features an overlook with a view of the Smoky Mountains.

Mouse Branch Trail mixes a single-track trail with old logging roads and passes through old homesites along its 6-mile course. You may see wildlife on the 8-mile Thompson Loop Trail. It crosses streams and passes through wildlife openings and old homesites. Check the trail-use schedule posted at the campground.

The boat ramp presents more recreational opportunities. You can fish Fontana Lake or access the Smokies. Cross the water and anchor in any cove on the Smokies' side of the lake. Then meander up the creek that created the cove and you will run into the Lakeshore Trail. It extends for miles in both directions. Many relics of the past may be seen, including stone walls, chimneys, and broken china. Make it an adventure. But remember, all artifacts are part of the park and must be left behind for others to enjoy.

Other facilities at Tsali include: a bike washing area for cleaning up after those long, muddy rides; a stable for horses; and a bank-fishing trail near the boat launch for safely wetting a line. If you need supplies, drive west on NC 28 to Wolf Creek General Store.

This is a fun area for active people. Use Tsali as a base camp and enjoy any and all of the activities available in this beautiful section of the Southern Appalachians.

To get there, from Bryson City take U.S. 19 south for 9 miles. Then turn right on NC 28 for 5.5 miles. Turn right again at the signed junction on FS 521 and follow it for 1.5 miles. Tsali Campground will be on your left.

KEY INFORMATION

Tsali Campground
Route 1, Box 16A
Robbinsville, NC 28771

Operated by: U.S. Forest Service

Information: (704) 479-6784

Open: April 14 to October 31

Individual sites: 41

Each site has: Tent pad, lantern post, picnic table, fire grate

Site assignment: First come, first served; no reservations

Registration: Self-registration on site

Facilities: Piped water, flush toilets, hot shower

Parking: At campsites only

Fee: $15 per night

Elevation: 1,750 feet

Restrictions:

Pets—On leash only

Fires—In fire rings only

Alcoholic beverages—At campsites only

Vehicles—None

Other—14-day stay limit

VANHOOK GLADE CAMPGROUND

Highlands, North Carolina

The very name *Vanhook Glade* conjures up images of relaxing in an open field surrounded by forest. This image is only partly true. Vanhook Glade *is* a relaxing place, but now the area and campground are completely reforested. The 20 sites are spread along a single paved loop well away from one another, mostly separated by a mature woodland of maple, oak, white pine, and hemlock, so characteristic of the Nantahala National Forest.

A side branch of the nearby Cullasaja River wends its way around the west side of the mountainside campground. The individual campsites are well leveled. A few of the sites actually have a short series of steps that go up or down to the camping area from the road, lending an added touch of intimacy. Short, graveled trails lead from the loop road to a comfort station in the loop's center, where a cold shower and flush toilets for each sex are available.

Tent camping is allowed at all the sites. Thirteen sites can accommodate a small RV or trailer. Since the camping is first come, first served, it's a matter of chance to find a site to fit your vehicle. Sites are usually available on weekdays, but if you want Vanhook for the weekend, get there early. Although very popular, the campground is rarely noisy, with no group camping and so few sites. However, if the wind is blowing

CAMPGROUND RATINGS

Beauty:	★★★★★
Site privacy:	★★★★
Site spaciousness:	★★★★
Quiet:	★★★
Security:	★★★★
Cleanliness/upkeep:	★★★★★

Vanhook Glade is ideally located in the middle of North Carolina's Falls Country.

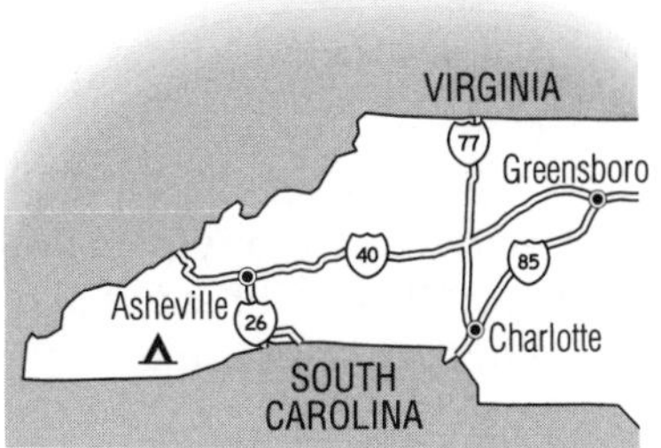

from the south, you can hear cars traveling on U.S. 64.

Four miles of deep woods divide the village of Highlands, over 4,000 feet in elevation, from Vanhook Glade. A short trip along U.S. 64 will bring you to this highbrowed, summer community with gift shops, restaurants, and even a few places to get camping supplies. Highlands is the point of origin for the Mountain Waters Scenic Byway, a 60-mile drive that winds through the Nantahala National Forest to the town of Almond, near Fontana Lake. The byway follows U.S. 64, old U.S. 64, North Carolina 1310, and U.S. 19.

Just out of Highlands you'll encounter the byway's first scenic feature, Bridal Veil Falls. You can actually drive your car under the 120-foot veil of water. Next, stop at Dry Falls. It's 3 miles west of Franklin. Take the .1-mile trail and descend to the falls. Then walk the trail that goes directly underneath the falls. You'll stay dry; that's how the falls got its name. West of Vanhook, U.S. 64 winds precariously through the 7-mile Cullasaja Gorge to the town of Franklin. Near Franklin is 250-foot Cullasaja Falls. Drive with care, as there is no safe pullover at the cascading falls. *Cullasaja* is Cherokee for "sweet water." These are but some of the attractions on the Mountain Waters Scenic Byway.

The nearby Cliffside Lake Recreation Area provides plenty of nonmotorized activities for anyone staying at Vanhook. It is located .2 mile west of Vanhook Glade. Cliffside Lake is the result of the damming of Skitty Creek. Try your luck with some trout, swim the brisk mountain water at the beach, or take a hike. The .7-mile Cliffside Loop Trail crosses the dam while circling the four-acre lake. Start at the picnic parking lot and take the 1.5-mile Clifftop Vista Trail. You'll come to a gazebo from the 1930s at the cliff top; from there view the surrounding Cullasaja River country. Come back down the Clifftop Nature Trail. Helpful interpretive signs detail the flora of the area. Skitty Creek Trail leads down to U.S. 64; it's an alternate route to Dry Falls. Take the 1.5-mile Homesite Road Trail down to U.S. 64. You can walk .4 mile west to Dry Falls or .4 mile east to Bridal Veil Falls; either way, be careful on the road. Don't feel like driving at all? Take the .3-mile Vanhook Trail. It accesses the Cliffside Lake area in combination with a short hike on Forest Service Road 57. The Vanhook Trail starts between campsites #6 and #7 in the campground.

Between the town of Highlands and Cliffside Lake there's enough to keep anyone busy. And the Vanhook Glade Campground literally sits in the middle of it all in North Carolina's Falls Country.

To get there, from Highlands drive west on U.S. 64 for 4.3 miles. Vanhook Glade Campground will be on your right.

KEY INFORMATION

Vanhook Glade Campground
Route 1, Box 247
Highlands, NC 28741

Operated by: U.S. Forest Service

Information: (704) 526-3765

Open: Mid-April to late October

Individual sites: 20

Each site has: Fire ring, picnic table, tent pad

Site assignment: First come, first served; no reservations

Registration: Self-registration on site

Facilities: Cold shower, flush toilets, pay phone

Parking: At campsites only

Fee: $8 per night

Elevation: 3,300 feet

Restrictions:

Pets—On 6-foot leash only

Fires—In fire rings only

Alcoholic beverages—At campsites only

Vehicles—Small campers and trailers only

Other—14-day stay limit

SOUTH CAROLINA CAMPGROUNDS

SOUTH CAROLINA

BURRELLS FORD CAMPGROUND

Walhalla, South Carolina

Before the Chattooga was declared a wild and scenic river, campers could drive all the way to Burrells Ford Campground. But since its inclusion as a wild and scenic river, a protective corridor has been established, effectively cutting off all direct auto access to the campground. This has been a mixed blessing: It has limited the use of the campground, but has cut maintenance as well. Of course, the short walk may deter some tent campers, but you can be guaranteed no RVs will ever be at Burrells Ford!

CAMPGROUND RATINGS

Beauty:	★★★★
Site privacy:	★★★★★
Site spaciousness:	★★★★★
Quiet:	★★★★★
Security:	★★★
Cleanliness/upkeep:	★★★

It's a 350-yard walk to this ultra primitive campground, but once here, the Chattooga Wild and Scenic River and Ellicott Rock Wilderness are just a few footsteps away.

Follow the old jeep road down to the river, entering the protected corridor. The road forks at the river bottom. The bottom is forested in tall white pines, with a thick understory of holly trees, rhododendron, and mountain laurel. The Chattooga runs shallow and clear directly in front of the campground, no doubt the ford of days gone by. On the other side of the river lies the state of Georgia, deeply shaded in thick, junglelike vegetation. Deep pools lie both up- and downstream of the campground, beckoning the camper to drop a line or take a dip. Rainbow and brown trout thrive in the mountain water.

The right fork of the old jeep road leads directly to the Chattooga. Campsites are spread along both sides of the road. Most sites are cooled beneath the shady canopy, but some lie in a glade that receives enough sun for grass to grow. All the sites

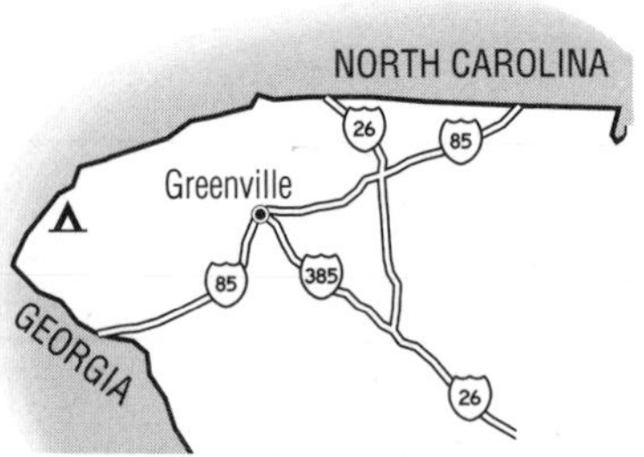

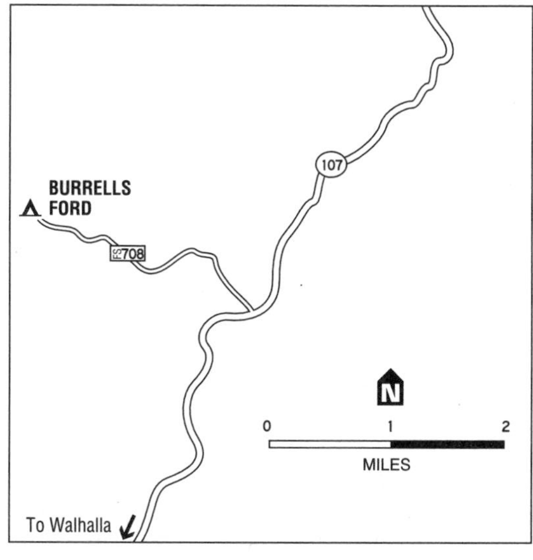

offer maximum privacy, as they are well away from one another. You'll never be able to carry enough stuff from your auto to the campground to utilize all the space offered at each campsite. Although, on my visit, one enterprising fellow toted his belongings down from the parking area in a wheelbarrow.

The left fork road enters the south side of the river bottom after crossing the clear and cool Kings Creek. Here you'll find more primitive sites: usually just a flat spot, a fire ring, and an occasional picnic table or lantern post. In a nearby flat, just upstream on Kings Creek, a very isolated site backs up against a steep hill for the tent camper seeking the ultimate in privacy. The left fork road intersects the Foothills Trail along the river; you'll encounter more informal sites there at about any inviting flat spot. Solitude is yours, to say the least.

As would be expected, amenities are minimal at Burrells Ford. Your arms will get a workout at the hand-pump well near the head of the campground. A pair of pit toilets are available for your comfort. This place is rustic. After all, it is within a wild and scenic river corridor and borders the Ellicott Rock Wilderness.

If you would like to see more of the attractive riverine ecosystem of the Chattooga, you only need to choose whether to go up or down the river. Down the Chattooga is the Foothills Trail. It winds along the river past Big Bend Falls for some 5 miles to Licklog Creek before turning southeast toward Oconee State Park. You can keep south along the river for 4.8 miles on the Chattooga Trail to Ridley Fields and SC 28. But first, tune up with a short .3-mile hike up Kings Creek to a woodsy waterfall, then return to camp.

Upstream and north from Burrells Ford, the Foothills Trail climbs away from the river along Medlin Mountain on its journey to Table Rock State Park nearly 70 miles away. If you stay north along the river, you'll soon enter the 7,000-acre Ellicott Rock Wilderness on the north section of the Chattooga Trail. It leads 4 scenic miles past riverside beaches to Ellicott Rock. This spot was selected in 1811 by a surveyor named Ellicott to designate the exact location where the Carolinas and Georgia came together. Stand on the rock and you can be in three states at once. Take the short side trail to Spoon Auger Falls on your way back.

It takes a little effort to reach Burrells Ford Campground, but you will be well rewarded. The Chattooga deserves its wild and scenic status, and the surrounding mountain lands are wild and scenic as well.

To get there, from Walhalla drive north on SC 28 for 8.5 miles to SC 107, then turn right. Follow SC 107 for 8.9 miles. Then turn left on gravel FS 708. Descend on FS 708 for 3 miles. Burrells Ford parking area will be on your left.

KEY INFORMATION

Burrells Ford Campground
Star Route
Walhalla, SC 29691

Operated by: U.S. Forest Service

Information: (864) 638-9568

Open: Year-round

Individual sites: 9

Each site has: Picnic table, fire ring, lantern post

Site assignment: First come, first served; no reservations

Registration: Not necessary

Facilities: Pit toilet, hand-pumped water

Parking: At Burrells Ford parking area

Fee: None

Elevation: 2,000 feet

Restrictions:

Pets—On leash only

Fires—In fire rings only

Alcoholic beverages—At campsites only

Vehicles—In parking area only

Other—Pack it in, pack it out

SOUTH CAROLINA

CHERRY HILL CAMPGROUND

Walhalla, South Carolina

Cherry Hill Campground is the focal point for the Cherry Hill Recreation Area. And it is a fine place to be—one of the best national forest campgrounds in the Southern Appalachians. The campground is located in the shallow, upper valley of West Fork Creek and lies covered with an abundant understory beneath a towering forest of hardwood and pine. The Forest Service must work hard to keep the vegetation from reclaiming this land.

Just off SC 107 is the entrance to Cherry Hill Campground. Immediately to the left is a circular turnaround, known as the overflow area. It once was home to a settler, whose chimney is still standing just off the loop; a short path leads to the ruins. Four new campsites have been carved into the woods up there, but you must park your car on the loop and carry your belongings. Not to worry, it is just a few feet from the loop to the new campsites.

The main campground lies beyond the overflow area on a short spur road that descends to tranquil West Fork Creek. Just past the self-service pay station are two isolated sites on their own mini-loop. A water spigot is nearby. Three other sites are located off the spur road before you reach the main loop.

The main loop makes a large oval beside the West Fork. All the sites along the West Fork are shrouded in rhododendron and are ideal for campers who like deep, lush

CAMPGROUND RATINGS

Beauty:	★★★★★
Site privacy:	★★★★
Site spaciousness:	★★★★★
Quiet:	★★★★
Security:	★★★★
Cleanliness/upkeep:	★★★★★

Cherry Hill is South Carolina's finest up-country campground.

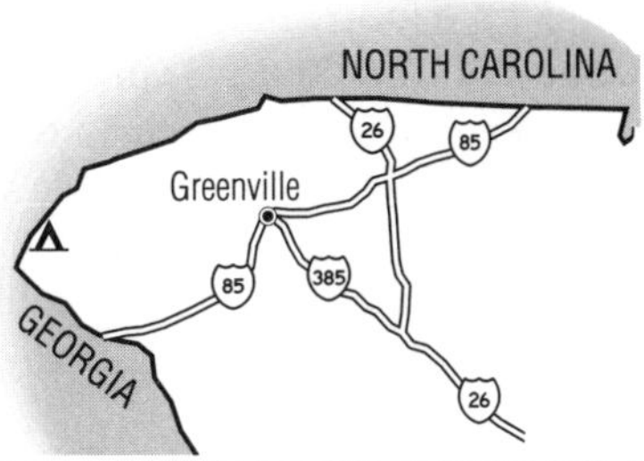

woods. Four relatively open sites are located on the inside of the main loop and offer a generous amount of space for even the most gear-laden camper. The sites away from the West Fork back against a hill beneath more open woods. Three water spigots are spread throughout the main loop. A clean, well-kept comfort station is at the north end of the loop; it has warm showers and flush toilets for each sex.

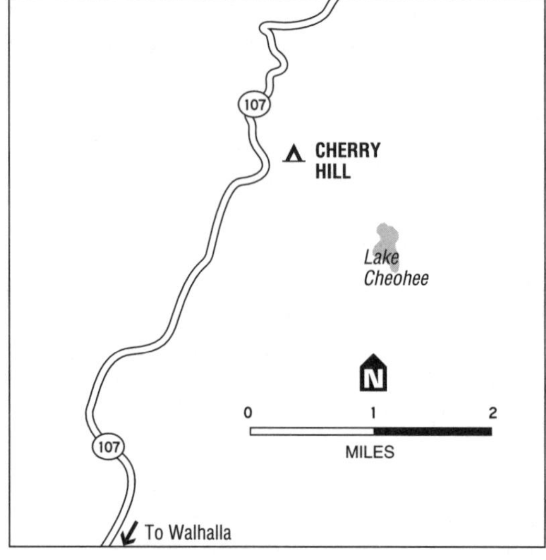

Near the comfort station, a small circle drive splits off the main loop. It holds four campsites with large parking areas, apparently designed for RVers; those were the only campers I saw at that spot during my visit. The circle has its own water spigot.

A campground host is stationed at Cherry Hill and keeps the place immaculate and safe. This only adds to the relaxing atmosphere of the area. Just as you get really comfortable, a notion will strike you to venture beyond your folding chair to explore more of the beauty of Sumter National Forest. And you don't even have to leave Cherry Hill to walk some of the area trails. The Cherry Hill Nature Trail is a good start. It leaves the campground and makes a half-mile loop among the ferns and brush of the white pine forest.

The Winding Stairs Trail also leaves from the campground. Follow it down as it switchbacks through an oak forest along the south side of the West Fork. I can only guess that the gentle switchbacking led to the Winding Stairs name. At any rate, after a mile, you'll come to a small but steep waterfall, as West Fork Creek has picked up some volume on its way to merge with Crane Creek. After the fall, the Winding Stairs Trail veers south to Crane Creek, then returns to West Fork only to end at 3.5 miles on Forest Service Road 710.

If you want bigger water, the Chattooga Wild and Scenic River is only a stroll away on the Big Bend Trail. The trail starts just across SC 107 from the campground and leads 2.7 miles west into the protected corridor of the Chattooga just above Big Bend Falls. From there, trails lead along the river in both directions for miles. Either way you go, you'll soon understand why this border river between South Carolina and Georgia is protected. The flora, fauna, and tumbling white water are yours to appreciate. And the fishing's good too.

Cherry Hill is a quality campground in an attractive forest setting. And for five bucks, it is a superlative value. Get all your supplies back in Walhalla, because once you're at Cherry Hill, you won't want to spoil your vacation with an early return to civilization.

To get there, from Walhalla drive north on SC 28 for 8.5 miles to SC 107, then turn right. Follow SC 107 for 7.5 miles. The entrance to Cherry Hill Campground will be on your right.

KEY INFORMATION

Cherry Hill Campground
Star Route
Walhalla, SC 29691

Operated by: U.S. Forest Service

Information: (864) 638-9568

Open: May to October

Individual sites: 28

Each site has: Picnic table, tent pad, fire pit, lantern post

Site assignment: First come, first served; no reservations

Registration: Self-registration on site

Facilities: Hot showers, flush toilets, piped water

Parking: At campsites only

Fee: $5 per night

Elevation: 2,250 feet

Restrictions:

Pets—On leash only

Fires—In fire pits only

Alcoholic beverages—At campsites only

Vehicles—None

Other—6 people per campsite

KEOWEE-TOXAWAY STATE PARK

Pickens, South Carolina

CAMPGROUND RATINGS

Beauty:	★★★★
Site privacy:	★★★★
Site spaciousness:	★★★★
Quiet:	★★★★
Security:	★★★★★
Cleanliness/upkeep:	★★★★★

Cherokee heritage, scenic hill country, mountain lakes, and a peaceful campground combine to make Keowee-Toxaway an outstanding state park experience.

This area of South Carolina is known as the Cherokee Foothills. And rightly so, for the Cherokee thrived here long before the white man ever laid eyes on this land. South Carolina recognized this, and Keowee-Toxaway celebrates Indian culture in the natural setting of the Cherokee at this quiet, well-maintained state park.

Tent campers can enjoy the area and return to a great campground. It is situated on a well-wooded knoll that tastefully integrates the campsites with the steep terrain using well-placed landscaping timbers. Shade is abundant beneath the canopy of hickories and oaks, though a relatively light understory somewhat diminishes privacy.

Tent campers have their own separate loop. No loud generators humming in the background will interfere with your listening to the birds chirp. The 14 tent sites are all spacious and level enough to set up a normal amount of gear, but expect some seriously sloping topography if you stray from your designated area. That very slope allows for balcony-like views into the hollows beyond the campground knoll. The campsites on the interior of the loop are less steep beyond their timbered camping area. The tent pads are among the finest I have seen. They are slightly crowned in the center, allowing for quick runoff during those heavy mountain thunderstorms. It is just one more obvious

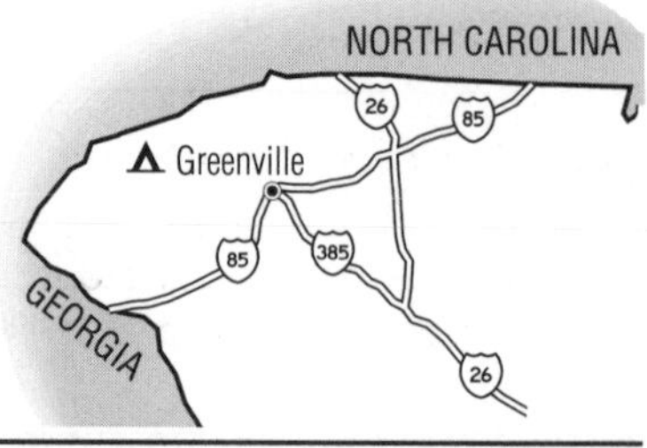

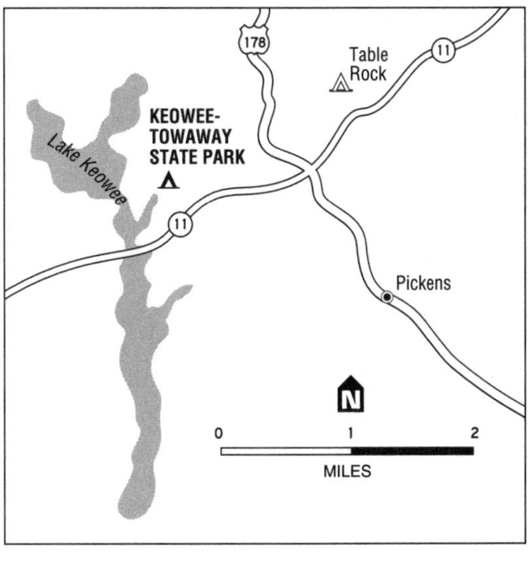

sign that the campground is well cared for.

You'll never have to go far for water. Three spigots are evenly distributed along the small loop. RVers and tenters share a comfort station located between the two separate loops. Hot showers and flush toilets are provided for each sex. Firewood is for sale at the park office. This may be the safest campground in the state. Park gates are locked at night and the ranger residence is just a stone's throw away from the tenters' loop.

Near the park office is the Cherokee Interpretive Center, which is the centerpiece recognizing the area's Cherokee heritage. During my visit I learned more about Cherokee life before, during, and after the arrival of European settlers. The center also tells of the flora and fauna that inhabit the state park. Visit the Interpretive Center first and you'll have an enhanced appreciation of the historic and natural life of Keowee-Toxaway.

Just outside the Interpretive Center is the quarter-mile Cherokee Interpretive Trail. It winds through the woods and chronicles the evolution of the Cherokee tribe at four informative kiosks, culminating with the story of their removal from their ancestral lands, known as the "Trail of Tears."

Other, longer trails carpet the park. The 4-mile Raven Rock Trail undulates amid the piney hills and hardwood hollows along clear creeks to a rock cliff overlooking Lake Keowee, then loops back via the Natural Bridge Trail to the park Meeting House. The rock bridge spans Poe Creek. The .7-mile Lake Trail leads from the campground down to the shore of Lake Keowee. This park may be only 1,000 acres, but South Carolinians make the most of the scenic beauty packed into the small package.

Lake lovers have two nearby bodies of water to enjoy. Both Lake Keowee and Lake Jocassee are clean waters backed against the Blue Ridge with mountainous shorelines. Lake Keowee is the larger of the two lakes. It is a warm-water fishery, with bass and bream as its primary sportfish. Anglers will be surprised to find trout in Lake Jocassee's deep, cool waters. Nearby Devils Fork State Park is on Lake Jocassee and offers quality camping as well, with a special section of walk-in tent sites.

You will find understated Keowee-Toxaway State Park a pleasant surprise. The campground is ideal for tent campers who want an intimate, well-kept campground with plenty of amenities. The blending of Cherokee heritage and natural beauty was a master stroke by South Carolina park officials. Don't make the mistake of overlooking this small jewel of the Palmetto State.

To get there, from Pickens drive north on U.S. 178 for 9 miles to SC 11. Turn left on SC 11 and drive for 7.9 miles to Keowee-Toxaway State Park.

KEY INFORMATION

Keowee-Toxaway State Park
108 Residence Drive
Sunset, SC 29685

Operated by: South Carolina State Parks

Information: (864) 868-2605

Open: Year-round

Individual sites: 14 for tents only

Each site has: Tent pad, picnic table, fire ring with attached grill

Site assignment: First come, first served; no reservations

Registration: Set up camp, register when ranger comes by

Facilities: Piped water, hot showers, flush toilets

Parking: At campsites only

Fee: $6 per night

Elevation: 1,000 feet

Restrictions:

Pets—On leash only

Fires—In fire rings only

Alcoholic beverages—Prohibited

Vehicles—None

Other—14-day stay limit

SOUTH CAROLINA

TABLE ROCK STATE PARK

Pickens, South Carolina

The distinctive granite face of Table Rock Mountain has attracted people to this scenic area since the days of the Cherokee, who believed the "Great Spirit" dined on the mountain's flat top, hence the name Table Rock. Later, this area was developed by the Civilian Conservation Corps during the Great Depression. The Corp's infrastructure handiwork was so well crafted that Table Rock Mountain State Park was placed on the National Register of Historic Places in 1989.

Not that this park needed humankind's imprint to be special. Waterfalls, deep forests, and rock outcrops adorned the mountains long before the 3,083 acres became a state park in 1935. The facilities just make it more user-friendly.

The campground suffices for the tent camper that likes to be on the move, but is not an end in itself. The main camping area has 75 sites spread on a two-loop setup in open, rolling woods that have suffered the ravages of many storms. These storms made pulp of the pine trees that once dotted the campground. In addition, little is left of the understory, minimizing privacy. It's strange to see a campground with electrical and water hookups at every campsite but no defined tent pads or elaborate site shaping. But don't let that scare you—only 20 of the sites are designated pull-through, which translates to RV.

CAMPGROUND RATINGS

Beauty:	★★★
Site privacy:	★★★
Site spaciousness:	★★
Quiet:	★★★
Security:	★★★★★
Cleanliness/upkeep:	★★★★★

Though Table Rock's campground may be average, the wide variety of attractions at this state park will make your stay worthwhile.

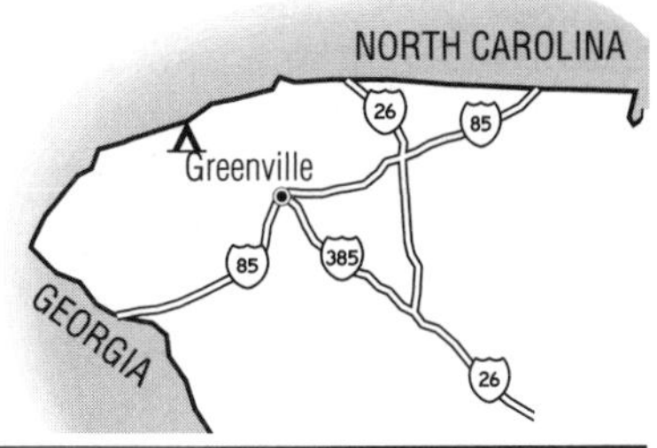

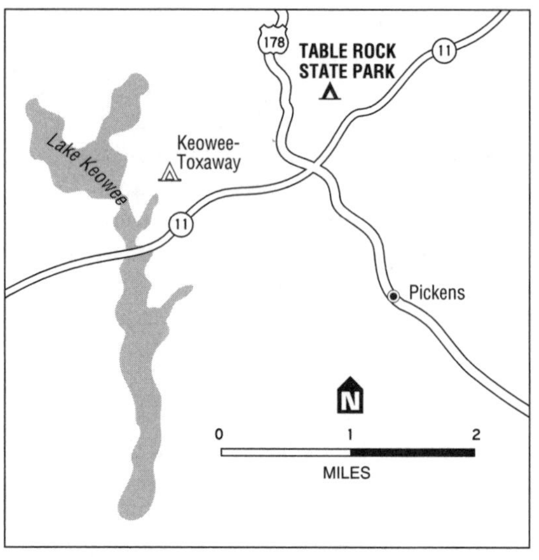

The first eight sites lie along the approach road and are very open. They are among the 25 specific sites that can be reserved. Unless you've been here you won't know the best sites to reserve, but don't let that deter you from coming.

Campsites are placed fairly close together once inside the loop. Three bathhouses with flush toilets and hot showers are evenly dispersed among the campsites, the exception being the sites on the approach road. A recreation building is in the center of the largest loop. Inside is a coin-operated laundry. Degrees of sun, shade, and slope vary from campsite to campsite. Plenty of level, shaded sites are available. Expect the best ones to be taken during the weekends. Don't be surprised if all 75 sites are filled and you are left to camp in the overflow area.

Located in thicker woods on a dead-end road, the overflow area may actually be preferable to the main camping area if you like less hustle and bustle. The 25 sites are spread along a loop and share a single bathhouse in the loop's center with flush toilets for each sex.

At Table Rock, the campground is just a place to rest and eat between activities. Two lakes lie within the park's confines. Pinnacle Lake finds summertime campers relaxing on its beach or jumping off the high and low diving boards into the clear, cool waters; canoers fishing for bass, bream, or catfish; and pedal boaters taking scenic rides atop the lake's 36 acres. Lake Oolenoy allows electric motors and has john boats for rent. Roam its 67 acres in search of the lunker bass. Or you can just toss a line from the fishing pier.

If water is not your thing, get together with the full-time park naturalist. Daily programs are offered during summer. The Table Rock Nature Center has displays that detail the natural history of the region. Children can have fun playing putt-putt or enjoying the playground equipment.

None of the above would be there if it weren't for the natural beauty of Table Rock. And the best way to enjoy these South Carolina mountain lands is on foot. A 10-mile trail network emanates from the Nature Center. The 3.4-mile Table Rock Trail lives up to its National Recreation Trail status. It leads upward among giant boulders to Pinnacle Ridge at Panther Gap. From Panther Gap, the trail climbs the steps of the Governor's Rock to reach the top of Table Rock at 3 miles. Hike another half mile to a wide view of the South Carolina countryside.

The Pinnacle Mountain Trail is very challenging. It passes Mill Creek Falls and Bald Rock on the way to the 3,425-foot peak, the park's highest point. A 2-mile connector trail links Pinnacle Mountain and Table Rock trails. The Carrick Creek Nature Trail offers a shorter 1.8-mile loop through forest characteristic of this worthwhile park.

To get there, from Pickens drive north on U.S. 178 for 9 miles. Turn right on SC 11 and follow it for 4.4 miles to West Gate Road. The park is a half mile up West Gate Road.

KEY INFORMATION

Table Rock State Park
246 Table Rock State Park Road
Pickens, SC 29671

Operated by: South Carolina State Parks

Information: (864) 878-9813

Open: Year-round

Individual sites: 100

Each site has: Water, electricity, picnic table, fire ring

Site assignment: 25 sites, reservations accepted; 75 sites, first come, first served

Registration: At camp store April to October; register with ranger rest of year

Facilities: Hot showers, camp store, laundry

Parking: At campsites only

Fee: $12 per night; $2 parking fee during summer

Elevation: 1,160 feet

Restrictions:

Pets—On leash only

Fires—In fire rings only

Alcoholic beverages—Prohibited

Vehicles—None

Other—14-day stay limit

GEORGIA CAMPGROUNDS

GEORGIA

AMICALOLA FALLS STATE PARK

Dawsonville, Georgia

Located in a saddle on Amicalola Mountain, Amicalola Falls Campground makes the most of its small perch, with 18 sites situated on the little flat ground that exists here at the southern end of North Georgia's highlands. Some sites are even dug into the hillsides. But all the sites on the small, gently rolling loop are level and kept camper-friendly by park staff.

Though the sites are segregated from one another, the lack of ground cover between sites minimizes privacy. However, the 16-foot trailer limit means it's mostly small groups of tent campers, which is unusual for a campground offering electricity and water at each site. The trailer size limit is due to the steep 22%-grade climb up Amicalola Mountain to the campground from the park Visitor Center along Little Amicalola Creek. Near at hand is a comfort station providing flush toilets, hot showers, two washers and dryers, and a soft-drink machine. A covered picnic area lies in the center of the camping loop. A park ranger lives on site at the small campground, providing the utmost in safety and information.

Adjacent to the campground, a field with a small, open amphitheater offers kids plenty of running room. Three playgrounds are located throughout the park. During the summer, ranger programs are offered every day, three times a day on weekends. Expect a full campground on

CAMPGROUND RATINGS

Beauty:	★★★★
Site privacy:	★★★
Site spaciousness:	★★★★
Quiet:	★★★★
Security:	★★★★★
Cleanliness/upkeep:	★★★★★

Amicalola Falls is the beginning of the Appalachian Trail and of your fun in the North Georgia mountains.

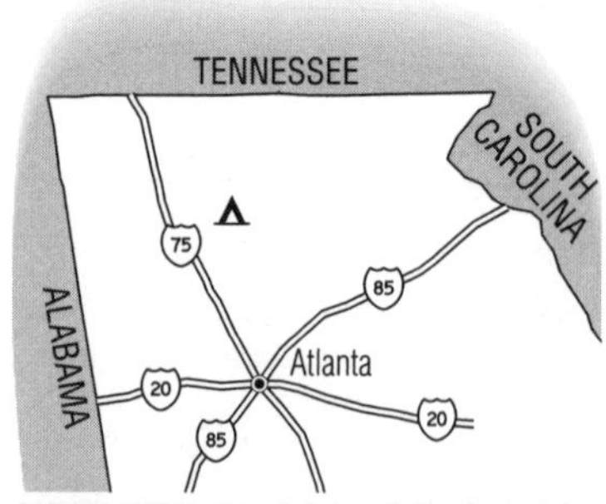

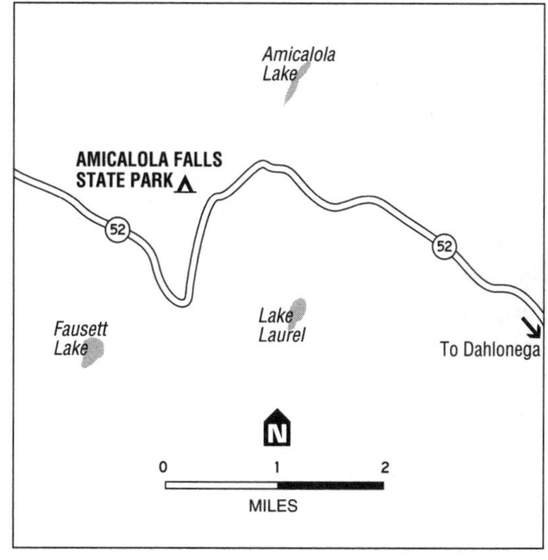

weekends, so reserve a site ahead of time. You cannot reserve a specific site, but after you make a reservation, some site will be available for you.

The high elevation and towering hardwoods keep the camp cool in the summer. This is an outstanding campground to enjoy fall colors. We came for the spring wildflower display. The cool spring delayed the blooms and the weather was windy and winter-like, so we spent most of our time huddled around the campfire commiserating with our fellow campers.

State parks are often named for an outstanding physical feature located within their boundaries. Centered around Amicalola Falls, this state park does more than just feature the highest waterfall in Georgia. Some claim it to be the highest cascade east of the Mississippi River. Whether the claim is true or not, the Cherokee word *Amicalola,* meaning "tumbling waters," is accurate. Check out the view from the top of the platform over the falls toward the hills and farmland of North Georgia. Then for a different perspective, take the Base of Falls Trail along Little Amicalola Creek from the Reflection Pool to the bottom of the falls. Look up at the seven cascades of water as they drop 729 feet.

Over 3 miles of hiking trails cover much of the park in both the high and low country. A 14-mile mountain biking trail loops into the nearby Chattahoochee National Forest and back to the park. Other recreational opportunities abound in the national forest, which abuts the state park. Inquire at the Visitor Center for maps and further information.

Amicalola Falls' biggest claim to fame is its proximity to the origin of the Appalachian Trail. The AT actually begins atop nearby Springer Mountain, but the 8.5-mile Approach Trail leading to Springer Mountain begins right behind the park's Visitor Center. Each spring, hundreds of would-be thru-hikers attempt to fulfill their dream of hiking from Georgia to Maine at this park. Taxis, families, and friends bring the ambitious to the park to begin their sojourn, following spring northward.

A little country store sits just outside the park boundary if you need supplies in a hurry; otherwise, drive back to Dawsonville, home of race car driver Bill Elliott. If you're hungry, go to the park lodge and enjoy the country buffet for breakfast, lunch, or dinner. Of course, afterwards, you'll have to go back to camp and enjoy a woodsy nap. And Amicalola Falls campground is just the place to take it.

To get there, from the old courthouse in Dawsonville, take GA 53 west for 2.4 miles. Turn right on GA 183 north for 10 miles to GA 52 east. Follow GA 52 east for 1 mile and turn left into Amicalola Falls State Park.

KEY INFORMATION

Amicalola Falls State Park
Star Route, Box 215
Dawsonville, GA 30534

Operated by: Georgia State Parks

Information: (404) 265-2885

Open: Year-round

Individual sites: 18

Each site has: Water spigot, electrical hookup, tent pad, fire ring, lantern post, grill

Site assignment: First come, first served after reservation is made

Registration: By reservation only, call (800) 864-PARK

Facilities: Flush toilets, hot showers, pay phone, soft-drink machine

Parking: At campsites only

Fee: $2 for Georgia Parks Pass, plus $15 per night; $17 per night in October; senior citizen discount of 20% off

Elevation: 2,750 feet

Restrictions:

Pets—On 6-foot leash only

Fires—In fire rings only

Alcoholic beverages—At campsites only

Vehicles—16-foot trailer length limit

GEORGIA

BLACK ROCK MOUNTAIN STATE PARK

Mountain City, Georgia

Black Rock Mountain Campground defies any campground stereotype—it has a 48-site campground with water, electricity, and cable TV hookups that is cram-packed with RVs, but on a dead-end road on a mountaintop rib ridge is an 11-site, walk-in, tents-only area that complements the rest of the worthwhile sights and activities of the state park. The 11 walk-in sites are the reasons this campground is in this book and these are the sites worth describing.

The walk-in sites are in three distinct areas. All sites are perched on the side of Black Rock Mountain wherever there is a hint of level ground. Some grading and site leveling have been done to make the sites camper-friendly. The mountain setting makes the sites incredibly appealing. Mix in some deep woods with far-off views, precipitous terrain, and a few cool breezes, and you have ridgetop tent camping at Black Rock Mountain State Park.

The main body of seven sites lies north of the parking area. Walk uphill and soon you'll come to the first two sites, set off a bit from the trail for privacy. Thick woods separate all the sites from one another. The next five sites extend farther up the ridge, yet none are so far that you can't tote whatever you normally bring on a tent camping expedition. Just think of it as a little work to achieve the maximum in scenery and solitude. Sites D and E are

CAMPGROUND RATINGS

Beauty: ★★★★★
Site privacy: ★★★★★
Site spaciousness: ★★★★
Quiet: ★★★
Security: ★★★★★
Cleanliness/upkeep: ★★★

Georgia's highest state park offers a tent-only camping section and plenty to see from atop Black Rock Mountain.

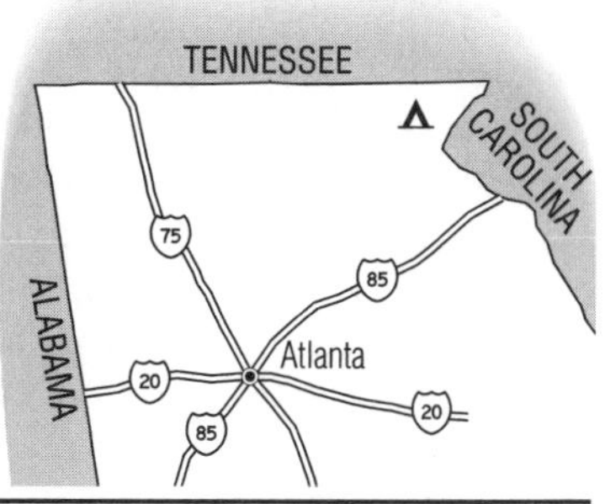

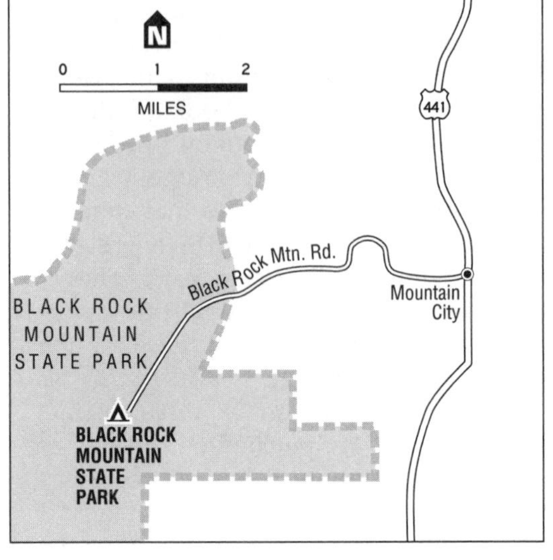

downhill from the parking area, on either side of their own trail. Sites A and B have their own parking area and are even more isolated than the rest. Still, it's just a short walk back to the comfort station.

The comfort station is located beside the parking area. Inside you'll find flush toilets, hot showers, and a dressing area for each sex. A water spigot is just outside the building. Ice, soft drinks, a washer and dryer, and a pay phone are back at the main campground. The Trading Post, which is the main campground store, has other supplies. That is the beauty of this setup: you can enjoy all these comforts but still camp in your own rustic atmosphere along with other tent campers.

Five mountains combine to make this the highest state park in Georgia. Black Rock gets its name from the sheer cliffs and outcrops of dark granite, called biotite-gneiss. For us that means open views of the Carolinas and Tennessee, as well as Georgia. Due to its high elevation, the mountaintop enjoys the same average summertime temperatures as Burlington, Vermont. Interestingly enough, the eastern continental divide splits the park. Water flowing off the north slope flows into the Mississippi and the Gulf of Mexico; the water from the south slope flows into the eastern seaboard of the Atlantic.

Speaking of water, there is a lake up there, too. You can fish 17-acre Black Rock Lake from the bank for bass, bream, catfish, and trout. Boating and swimming are not allowed.

However, the most popular activity at Black Rock is hiking. Start out on the short Ada-Hi Falls Trail. The trail dips into a cool cove about .2 mile on the way to the falls. Since the trail and creek are so high on the mountain, there is not a whole lot of water to work with. Still, the trail will give you a taste of high-country woods.

Next, take on the 2.2-mile loop Tennessee Rock Trail. It swings through varied types of forest and tops out at the 3,640-foot peak of Black Rock Mountain. But the best view is a short ways farther at Tennessee Rock. Look both ways at the countryside around you.

We came in late May; the high mountains around us offered varying tints of green as spring made its way up their crests. The valleys below were deep green. The shades became lighter with the rise in elevation. Tennessee Rock is a good place to catch a sunset. Another rewarding trek is the James E. Edmonds Trail, a 7.2-mile backcountry loop that traverses the north end of the park. A highlight of this trail is the view from Lookoff Mountain.

You'll find that Lookoff Mountain is only one of the many sights of this highland sanctuary in the North Georgia mountains.

To get there, from Mountain City take Black Rock Mountain Road west off U.S. 441 for 3 miles. The road dead-ends at the park.

KEY INFORMATION

Black Rock Mountain State Park
P.O. Drawer A
Mountain City, GA 30562

Operated by: Georgia State Parks

Information: (706) 746-2141

Open: Year-round

Individual sites: 11, walk-in tents only; 48, RVs and tents

Each site has: Tent pad, picnic table, lantern post, fire ring

Site assignment: May choose preferred site if available

Registration: Call (800) 864-PARK; reservations must be made at least 2 days prior to arrival; persons without reservations are guaranteed a one-night stay only

Facilities: Piped water, flush toilets, hot showers

Parking: At parking area for walk-in sites

Fee: $2 Georgia Parks Pass, plus $10 per night

Elevation: 3,040 feet

Restrictions:

Pets—On leash at all times

Fires—In fire rings only; must be attended at all times

Alcoholic beverages—At campsites only

Vehicles—None

GEORGIA

CLOUDLAND CANYON STATE PARK

Trenton, Georgia

Cloudland Canyon is another example of a state stepping in and preserving a special slice of nature for all of us to enjoy. Sure, Cloudland Canyon has been developed to a degree, but part of that development consists of three campgrounds, including one delightful one for tents only. The facilities augment the natural state of things on Lookout Mountain, where Sitton Gulch Creek has carved a gorge on the mountain's western edge, allowing vistas from the rim of the gorge into the lands below.

Atop Lookout Mountain, the waters of Daniel Creek and Bear Creek cut their own gorges into the land before converging to form Sitton Gulch Creek. It is between these two creeks that the East Rim Campground lies. East Rim has 24 campsites spread along a loop that meanders beneath a second-growth, pine-oak forest that is commonly found on the mountaintop. Many of the sites have drive-through parking areas. That means RVs. All campsites have water and electrical hookups. A bathhouse with hot showers centers the loop. Many of the park's developed amenities are nearby. This campground may be appropriate for families with young children.

The West Rim Campground is located across Daniel Creek, away from the main section of the park. The mixed forest there is fairly thick, with second-growth trees

CAMPGROUND RATINGS

Beauty:	★★★★
Site privacy:	★★★★
Site spaciousness:	★★★★
Quiet:	★★★
Security:	★★★★★
Cleanliness/upkeep:	★★★★

Georgia's most gorge-ous state park has a tent-only campground to match the scenery.

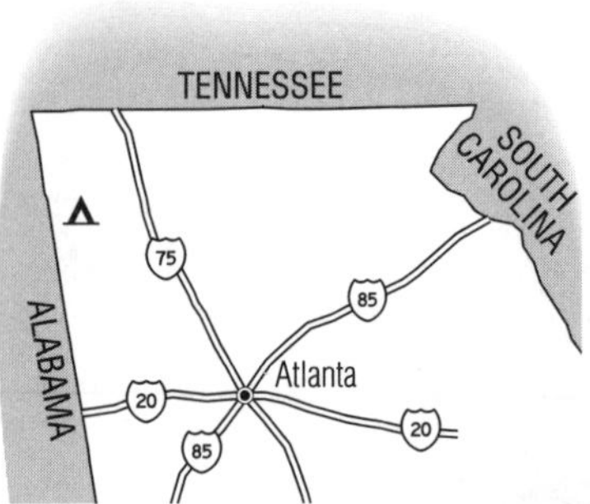

competing with each other on a slight slope. The 48 spacious sites are spread along two loops. An understory of young hardwoods provides much privacy between sites, each of which offers water and electrical hookups. Each loop has a comfort station with flush toilets and hot showers.

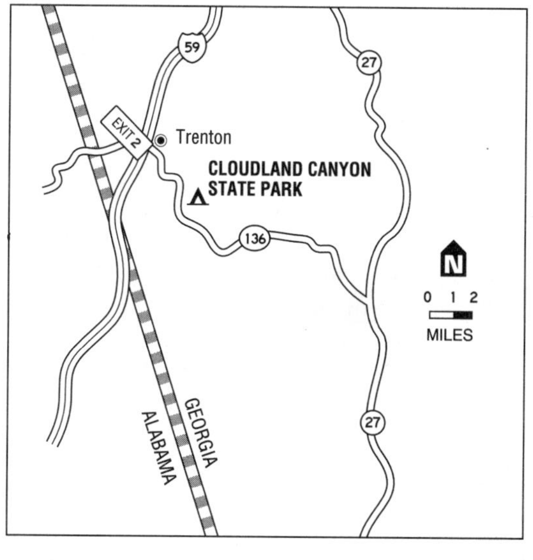

The Walk-In Campground is by far the best. Why? First, it allows tents only. Second, it is farthest from the rest of the park developments. Third, it is well laid out in a handsome, forested setting. Park your vehicle in the Walk-In Campground parking area. The campsites are spread along a looping footpath on gently rolling terrain. The farthest sites are three-fourths of a mile from the parking area—and are worth every step.

Each site is set off in the woods, availing the maximum in site privacy. There is ample room to spread out any gear you may carry. A short trail bisects the campground to access the comfort station, with its hot showers and flush toilets. The atmosphere is of camping in the woods, not of being in a campground with a few trees around.

Cloudland Canyon wouldn't be a state park if it didn't have natural beauty to begin with. Our visit here was particularly scenic. Fall had reached Lookout Mountain. Colorful maples and oaks mingled with the pine trees. The air was brisk. The skies were clear. We knew the views would be inspiring. We set out on the 4.9-mile West Rim Loop Trail, crossing Daniel Creek and skirting the rim of the Daniel Creek Gorge. The trail continued along the main gorge, where overlooks afforded views into the three canyons formed by

Daniel Creek, Bear Creek, and Sitton Gulch Creek. We could see the point where the three gorges met, with a blaze of fall color crowning the rim.

The views continued. Below, we could see the town of Trenton. The trail left the canyon rim beyond the last overlook and re-entered the mountaintop wood. Eventually we came to the side trail that accessed the Walk-In Campground; we returned to our camp for a hot cup of coffee. Later, we took the short trail to the park's two waterfalls on Daniel Creek. Being autumn, the creek was low on water; yet we enjoyed our walk just the same.

There is still another trail: the Backcountry Loop. It follows Bear Creek and the east rim. You have to step out to find your own overlooks, so be careful. The trail requires crossing a footbridge that is often out from floods. Inquire at the park office for the status of this trail.

Alternative activities include tennis and swimming. Lighted courts are available for day or evening use, and the pool is open from Memorial Day to Labor Day. Children can enjoy the park's playground.

Still, this is primarily a nature lover's place. And at Cloudland Canyon State Park, there is plenty to love.

To get there, from Trenton and I-59, take GA 136 for 8 miles up to Lookout Mountain. Cloudland Canyon State Park will be on your left.

KEY INFORMATION

Cloudland Canyon State Park
Route 2, Box 150
Rising Fawn, GA 30738

Operated by: Georgia State Parks

Information: (706) 657-4050

Open: Year-round

Individual sites: 30, walk-in, tents only; 75, tent and trailer

Each site has: Picnic table, tent pad, fire ring; tent and trailer sites have electricity and water hookups

Site assignment: May choose preferred site if available

Registration: Call (800) 864-PARK; reservations must be made at least 2 days prior to arrival; persons without reservations are guaranteed a one-night stay only

Facilities: Hot showers, flush toilets, phone, soft-drink machine

Parking: At campsites only

Fee: $2 Georgia Parks Pass, plus $13 per night, $8 per night for walk-in sites

Elevation: 1,800 feet

Restrictions:

Pets—On 6-foot leash only

Fires—In fire rings only

Alcoholic beverages—Prohibited

Vehicles—None

Other—14-day stay limit

GEORGIA

DESOTO FALLS CAMPGROUND

Cleveland, Georgia

Where do the names Desoto and Frogtown come together? The answer is at Desoto Falls Campground, which is located along the banks of Frogtown Creek in the 650-acre Desoto Falls Scenic Area. The sylvan campground provides a good base camp from which to enjoy the scenery of the falls, as well as the nearby Appalachian Trail and Raven Cliffs Wilderness.

With a campground this nice it may be hard to tear yourself away. The 24 large campsites are split among two creekside loops arranged beneath a dense forest of deciduous and evergreen trees. It is one of the most densely forested campgrounds I've ever seen. This dense forestation makes each site seem like an island unto itself and the campground seem more diffused than it really is.

The upper loop has a small stream running between the very spacious and private sites, which are separated by thick cover. Four low-volume flush toilets and two drinking faucets are interspersed in the loop. Seven sites border Frogtown Creek but are far enough back to be out of the flood-prone areas. The intonations of the creek can be heard throughout the campground.

The lower loop has a campground host for campers' security. It also has several creekside sites. In the center of the loop is a modern rest room facility with warm showers. Two drinking fountains with

CAMPGROUND RATINGS

Beauty:	★★★★
Site privacy:	★★★★★
Site spaciousness:	★★★★★
Quiet:	★★★
Security:	★★★★
Cleanliness/upkeep:	★★★★

The heavily wooded Desoto Falls Campground is well located for exploring the central Chattahoochee National Forest.

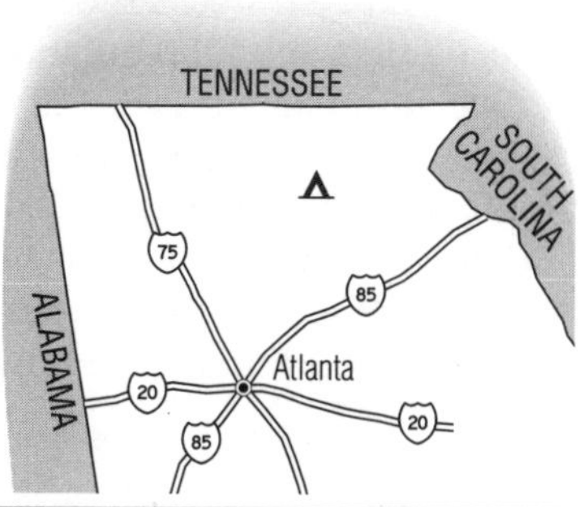

connecting faucets complete this deluxe package.

The primary attractions of this scenic area are the three falls located at intervals along Frogtown Creek. Why the name Desoto? According to legend, early settlers found a strange piece of armor at the base of the falls. It was supposedly left behind by Hernando de Soto himself as he hunted for gold. Nearby Dahlonega actually did experience America's first gold rush in the 1830s.

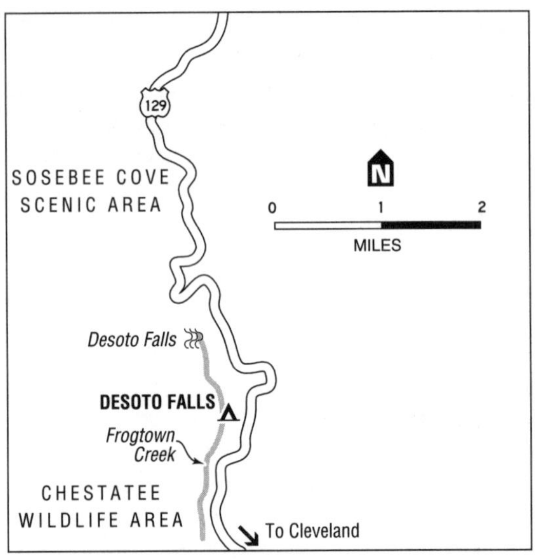

The three falls of Frogtown Creek are natural treasures. The trail to the falls starts from the lower camping loop. Follow Frogtown Creek downstream .2 mile to view the Lower Falls drop some 35 feet onto the rocks below. Return upstream, past the campground, .7 mile to the Middle Falls with its four-stage, 90-foot drop. The trail steepens the last mile beyond the Middle Falls to the Upper Falls, which is a 200-foot slide.

Frogtown Creek and its tributaries offer quality trout fishing. Georgia Game and Fish stocks the stream weekly during the summer. Nearby Waters Creek offers special regulation trophy trout fishing.

Just 1.5 miles up U.S. 129 is Neels Gap and the Appalachian Trail. Either way you hike you are in for a treat. We went both directions during our trip to the area. The wind blew hard during the 2.5-mile westward pull to the top of Blood Mountain. But the view from the highest point of the AT in Georgia was worth it. The rock outcrop of Blood Mountain, at 4,458 feet, enabled us to see far south into Georgia, as clouds scudded overhead.

We returned to Neels Gap for lunch, then headed east. First we passed Walasiyi, the state-owned hiking and gift shop. After perusing the unusual ridgetop store, we hiked into the Raven Cliffs Wilderness. The trail wound along the crest until we came to our destination at my favorite peak in Georgia, Cowrock Mountain. With a name like that, it had to be worth hiking 5 miles to see. And it was. The rock-overlaid peak offered views westward into the Boggs Creek watershed and summit after summit beyond that. We returned fulfilled to Neels Gap, then drove to Cleveland and devoured a well-deserved pizza that induced a sound night's rest back at the campground.

Towns Creek Trail (Forest Trail #131) and Dodds Creek Trail (FT #22) are two other pathways that lead into the heart of the 8,000-acre Raven Cliffs Wilderness. If you would like to know more about America's first gold rush, drive 4 miles south on U.S. 129 to U.S. 19, and then drive 12 miles to Dahlonega. The theme of this mountain town is the gold rush. They have some of the typical tourist traps, but also some worthwhile historic buildings and displays.

To get there, head north on U.S. 129 from Cleveland for 15 miles. Desoto Falls Recreation Area will be on your left.

KEY INFORMATION

Desoto Falls Campground
1015 Tipton Drive
Dahlonega, GA 30523

Operated by: U.S. Forest Service

Information: (706) 864-6173

Open: May to October

Individual sites: 24

Each site has: Tent pad, picnic table, fire ring, lantern post

Site assignment: First come, first served; no reservations

Registration: Self-registration on site

Facilities: Warm showers, flush toilets, piped water, drinking fountains

Parking: At campsites only

Fee: $6 per day

Elevation: 2,080 feet

Restrictions:

Pets—On leash only

Fires—In fire rings only

Alcoholic beverages—At campsites only

Vehicles—22-foot trailer length limit

Other—14-day stay limit

GEORGIA

DOCKERY LAKE CAMPGROUND

Dahlonega, Georgia

CAMPGROUND RATINGS

Beauty:	★★★★★
Site privacy:	★★★★
Site spaciousness:	★★★★★
Quiet:	★★★★
Security:	★★★★★
Cleanliness/upkeep:	★★★★

Relax in the highland campground beside the quiet waters of crystal-clear Dockery Lake.

An exceptional campground beside a trout-filled lake beneath the shadow of the Appalachian Trail. And that is only the beginning of Dockery Lake Campground. Set in a large cove on the southern shore of three-acre Dockery Lake, this campground is as aesthetically pleasing as its natural mountain surroundings of the Cedar Ridge Mountain Range. The sites are landscaped using native stones with plenty of trees and groundcover that blend in well with the upland landscape. The tent pads are bordered in concrete with gravel pebbles for drainage. Not much leveling was needed, as the slope of the campground is negligible.

The sites are arranged on either side of a one-way gravel road, beneath a pine and hardwood forest, with an understory of hemlock and mountain laurel. Five sites lie directly lakeside; the other six are only yards away but have the advantage of being high enough to overlook the lake. At the campground's end, a retaining wall encloses a small grassy area beside the lake, producing an ideal spot for fishing, sunbathing, or just relaxing.

Two combination water fountain/spigots are positioned about the campground, and a comfort station with flush toilets for either sex stands on the uphill side of the campground. The campground host resides at the campground's center, adding an element of security for everyone. The

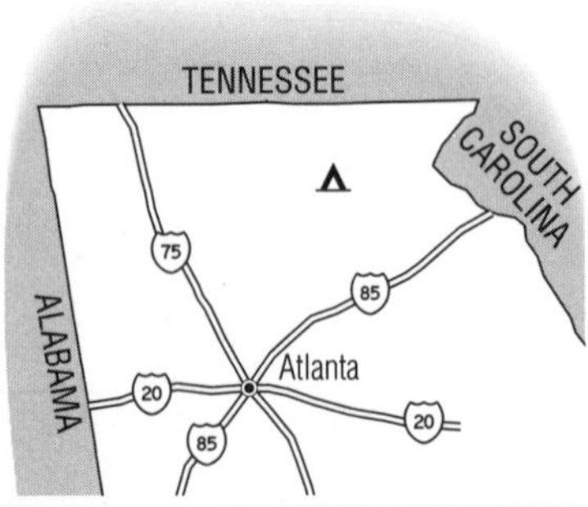

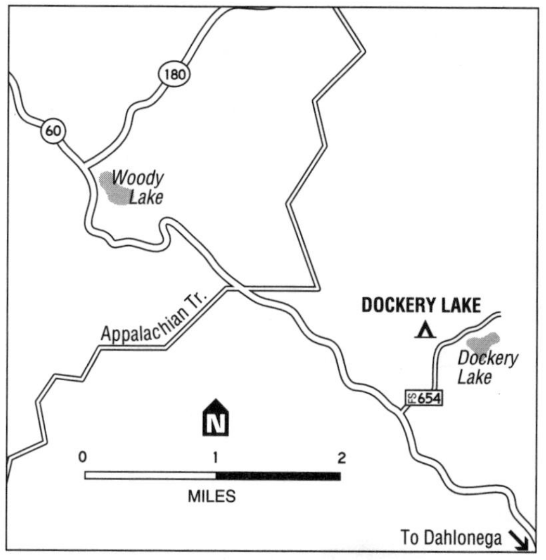

intimate lakeside environment spells vacation for any camper whose destination is Dockery Lake.

Dockery Lake is fed from the chilly headwaters of Waters Creek, tumbling off the slopes of Jacobs Knob along the Appalachian Trail. The pure water is cold enough to support a healthy population of trout, so it comes as no surprise that fishing is a popular pastime at Dockery Lake. The lake is stocked on a regular basis by the Georgia Department of Natural Resources. Anglers can be found here using a rod and reel lakeside or in a canoe or other small craft. No motors are allowed, however. The .6-mile Lakeshore Trail snakes around the lake. Short side trails lead to platforms at the water's edge, providing good fishing or lake-viewing spots. A wooden platform with handrails sits over the small dam. It's a good vantage point for lake enthusiasts to take in the entire six acres of the crystalline body of water. The trail is graveled throughout the campground.

The one-way gravel road bisecting the campground leads a short distance to the picnic parking area. It is there that the Dockery Lake Trail begins. It leads 3.4 miles up to Miller Gap and the Appalachian Trail. Look for deer and grouse feeding in the shadows. After a mile of trail treading along tributaries of Waters Creek, you'll be lower than when you started. The trail climbs for the remainder of its journey to Miller Gap, just shy of 3,000 feet. It is 2.9 miles west on the AT to Woody Gap and GA 60. It is just over 5 miles east to Blood Mountain, at 4,458 feet, the highest point of the AT in Georgia.

For a scenic overview of the surrounding mountains, drive back to GA 60 and turn right. A quarter-mile on your right is the Chestatee Overlook, a cleared area offering a vista of the Chattahoochee National Forest to the east. Another mile up GA 60 is Woody Gap and a view of the Yahoola Valley. The AT passes through the grassy gap. If you need supplies, drive back to Dahlonega.

To get there, from Dahlonega take GA 60 north for 12 miles. Turn right at the sign for Dockery Lake on FS 654 for 1 mile.

KEY INFORMATION

Dockery Lake Campground
1015 Tipton Drive
Dahlonega, GA 30533

Operated by: U.S. Forest Service

Information: (706) 864-6173

Open: April 19 to October 30

Individual sites: 11

Each site has: Tent pad, fire ring, picnic table, lantern post

Site assignment: First come, first served; no reservations

Registration: Self-registration on site

Facilities: Flush toilets, water spigots

Parking: At campsites

Fee: $5 per night

Elevation: 2,400 feet

Restrictions:

Pets—On leash only

Fires—In fire rings only

Alcoholic beverages—At campsites only

Vehicles—22-foot trailer length limit

Other—14-day stay limit

GEORGIA

FORT MOUNTAIN STATE PARK

Chatsworth, Georgia

Fort Mountain is the site of an unexplained mystery. A strange, serpentine rock wall sits atop the mountain, bounded on both sides by sheer cliffs. The wall, ranging from 2 to 6 feet in height, spans 855 feet and is broken with circular pits at 30-foot intervals, hence the name Fort Mountain. No one is sure who built it, or for what purpose, but it is speculated that the wall was some kind of fortification, or was somehow related to religious activities. Either way, it is listed in the National Register of Historic Places. Later, thanks to the land donation of Ivan Allen in 1929, far-sighted Georgians also saw the natural beauty of the area and established a state park.

Surrounded on all sides by the Chattahoochee National Forest, Fort Mountain State Park has two splendid family campgrounds that offer a variety of campsites. Set in a hardwood forest on a rolling mountainside, there are 70 shady RV/tent sites, each with water and electricity. For the more primitive tent camper, four sites with water but no electricity are available. In addition, five walk-in "squirrel's nests" offer a level site for tents only. This campground has a lot of guidelines in regard to RV size for certain campsites, but, unless you like to disregard guidelines, they will work in your favor. If you have any questions, call ahead; reservations are strongly recommended.

CAMPGROUND RATINGS

Beauty:	★★★★★
Site privacy:	★★★
Site spaciousness:	★★★
Quiet:	★★★★
Security:	★★★★★
Cleanliness/upkeep:	★★★★★

The mysterious rock wall on top of Fort Mountain is just one reason to explore one of Georgia's finest state parks.

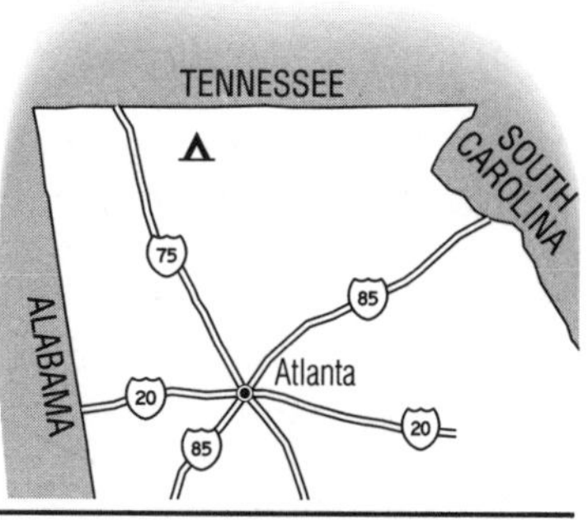

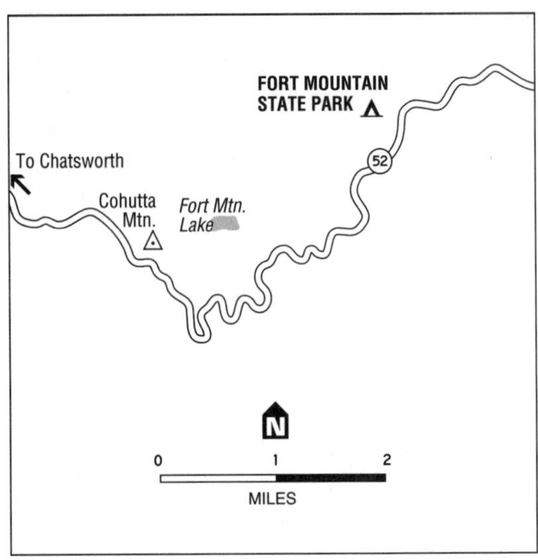

Fort Mountain State Park is peaceful and safe. Quiet hours are strictly enforced. The park gates are locked between 10 P.M. and 7 A.M. The park office is staffed from 8 A.M. to 5 P.M. by accommodating park personnel. Three pay phones, three coin laundries, and a dump station provide campers with convenience. Get your supplies in Chatsworth before you drive up the mountain, as there are no nearby stores in the high country.

You'll find plenty to do without ever leaving the park. A 17-acre, spring-fed lake offers fishing and a swimmer's beach complete with bathhouse. Tool around the lake in pedal boats or fishing boats, which are available for rent. For the kids, there is a playground and miniature golf course. Scheduled programs, presented by a park naturalist, are offered Wednesday through Sunday during the summer.

Naturally, Fort Mountain has trails. Near the campground, the 1.2-mile Lake Trail loops the lake. Nearby, the Big Rock Nature Trail offers a cliff-edge view off the mountain, halfway along its half-mile loop. Beyond the park office is the 1.8-mile Old Fort Trail that leads to the 855-foot-long stone wall.

Was the wall a religious site or a defensive barrier to ward off neighboring tribes? Currently, many embrace the wall's possible religious significance. The wall runs east-west, and many speculate that an unknown tribe of sun-worshipping Indians built it. But Cherokee legend points to the wall being erected by a group of light-skinned, "moon-eyed people" who could see in the dark. The "moon-eyed people" may have been led by the Welsh explorer Madoc, who supposedly came north from Mobile Bay in the 14th century. Or was it built by Hernando de Soto as a defense against Indian attacks, while he searched for silver and gold? Or was it something else altogether? Explore the wall and decide for yourself.

Take the side trail to the 60-year-old lookout tower, originally built from natural materials during the Great Depression, then refurbished in the 1970s. The mountains of North Georgia and East Tennessee stand out on the horizon. Hike to the overlook deck west of the stone tower and you will see just how far it is down to the Conasauga River valley below. The really adventurous can attempt the 8.2-mile loop trail that encircles the campground. With such a quality campground situated amid spring wildflowers, summer's lush greenery, fall colors, and winter's clarity, it's no mystery that Fort Mountain State Park is a year-round attraction.

To get there, from Chatsworth turn east on GA 52. Drive 7 miles up into the Cohutta Range. Fort Mountain State Park will be on your left.

KEY INFORMATION

Fort Mountain State Park
181 Fort Mountain Park Road
Chatsworth, GA 30705

Operated by: Georgia State Parks

Information: (706) 695-2621

Open: Year-round

Individual sites: 79

Each site has: Water, electrical hookups, picnic table, lantern post

Site assignment: May choose preferred site if available

Registration: Call (800) 864-PARK; reservations must be made at least 2 days prior to arrival; persons without reservations are guaranteed a one-night stay only

Facilities: Water, electrical hookups, hot showers, flush toilets

Parking: At campsites only

Fee: $2 Georgia Parks Pass, plus $14 per night, $8 per night for walk-in sites with water only

Elevation: 2,800 feet

Restrictions:

Pets—On 6-foot leash only

Fires—In fire rings only

Alcoholic beverages—At campsites only

Vehicles—Maximum 2 vehicles per site

GEORGIA

LAKE CONASAUGA CAMPGROUND

Chatsworth, Georgia

CAMPGROUND RATINGS

Beauty:	★★★★★
Site privacy:	★★★★
Site spaciousness:	★★★★
Quiet:	★★★★
Security:	★★★★
Cleanliness/upkeep:	★★★★

Camp, fish, and hike in the high country around Georgia's highest lake.

Set in the rugged highlands of the western Chattahoochee National Forest, 19-acre Lake Conasauga is a mountaintop oasis adjacent to the 34,000-acre Cohutta Wilderness, Georgia's largest wilderness area. Tent campers will be well rewarded after the long gravel drive that deters all but the most determined RVers. Expect a nearly full campground on weekends. Make sure to bring everything you need—civilization is far away. After you go boating, hiking, swimming, fishing, and wildlife viewing, you will be ready to kick back in the breezy campground.

The campground is located near the lake and divided into three areas. The main campground has 31 sites divided into two loops. The upper loop is on a forested ridge with 12 spacious and private sites. It has several water spigots and a central bathroom atop the ridge with flush toilets for each sex. The lakeside lower loop is shaded by white pine with little understory. Five sites are actually lakefront. Those and the other sites offer an appealing view of the clear blue waters ringed in rhododendron. A comfort station and water spigot are located at the head of the loop.

The second loop area holds only four sites in a grassy clearing ringed with trees, but no view of the lake. But the Lakeshore Trail makes the lake instantly accessible.

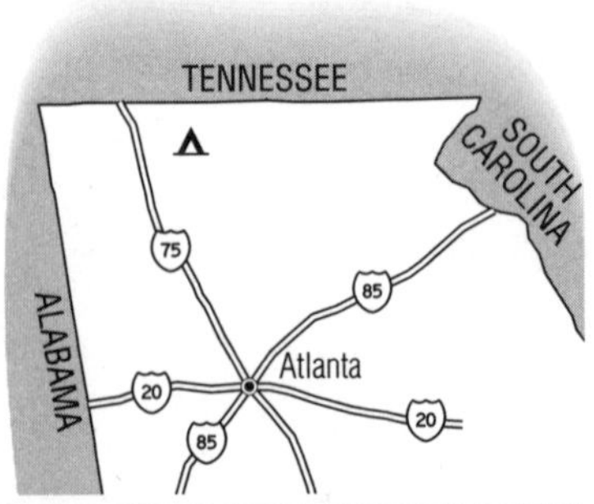

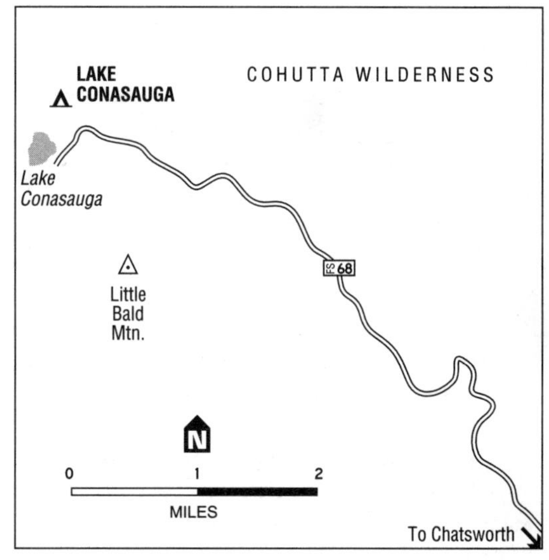

Flush toilets and water are nearby. This small area has an isolated feel to it.

The final five sites sit in the overflow area atop the ridge above the lake. The area has flush toilets but no water, though a short trip to the other loops can amend that problem. The breezes are stronger here, and the area has a mountaintop feel to it. A campground host is located at the largest loop on summer weekends. Recycling stations are in each camping area.

If you find it hard to pick a site, you will really be hard-pressed to decide what to do first. To explore Lake Conasauga, dammed in 1940 by the CCC, you can take the .8-mile Lakeshore Trail that courses through hemlock and rhododendron along the water's edge. A grassy glade with benches covers the dam. Sit down, relax, and absorb the atmosphere. Or use a canoe or small johnboat and fish for bream, bass, or trout. Only electric motors are allowed. Want to take a dip? Across the lake from the campground is a ringed-off swimming beach. You can reach it from the picnic area or the Lakeshore Trail.

Start hiking right from your campsite. The Songbird and Grassy Mountain Trails are instantly accessible. Wildlife viewing is made easy by the .6-mile Songbird Trail. The Forest Service has cleared small plots along the trail to make a better habitat for the likes of the owl, woodcock, and kingfisher. Beavers have dammed the trailside stream, strengthening biodiversity with their ponds that provide a habitat for numerous amphibians. The 2-mile Grassy Mountain Tower Trail climbs gradually to the 3,692-foot fire tower.

From the tower you can see the forested Cohutta Wilderness and the Southern Appalachians as they stretch northward into Tennessee.

Just a short distance away from Lake Conasauga are forest roads that circle the southern half of the Cohutta Wilderness. No fewer than six trails lead from these roads into the heart of the Cohutta. Make the most of your adventuring with a map of the wilderness, which can be obtained at the Ranger Station in Chatsworth. The Tearbritches Trail (Forest Trail #9) starts just east of the campground. It crosses Bald Mountain then descends to Bray Field along the Conasauga River. The Conasauga River has a reputation as Georgia's cleanest, clearest waterway. Chestnut Lead Trail (FT #11) drops into the lower Conasauga in 1.8 miles. East Cowpen Trail (FT #30) traverses the high country at the heart of the wilderness. Large trees, wildlife, and good fishing are Cohutta hallmarks.

Conasauga is an area of Georgian superlatives: the highest lake, the cleanest water, the largest wilderness. Come here with high expectations. You won't be disappointed.

To get there, from Chatsworth take U.S. 411 north for 4 miles; turn right at the traffic light in Eton. Follow FS 18 east for 10 miles. Turn left on FS 68 and follow it for 10 miles. Lake Conasauga will be on your right.

KEY INFORMATION

Lake Conasauga Campground
401 Old Ellijay Road
Chatsworth, GA 30705

Operated by: U.S. Forest Service

Information: (706) 695-6736

Open: April 15 to October 31

Individual sites: 40

Each site has: Fire ring, picnic table, lantern post, tent pad

Site assignment: First come, first served; no reservations

Registration: Self-registration on site

Facilities: Flush toilets, piped water

Parking: At campsites only

Fee: $5 per night

Elevation: 3,150 feet

Restrictions:

Pets—On leash only

Fires—In fire rings only

Alcoholic beverages—At campsites only

Vehicles—22-foot trailer length limit

Other—14-day stay limit

GEORGIA

TATE BRANCH CAMPGROUND

Clayton, Georgia

Tate Branch is a small, streamside campground nestled far back in the mountains of North Georgia. Tate Branch flows through the campground into the unspoiled Tallulah River, which provides a panoramic backdrop for your time at Tate Branch. Near the appealing campground are fishing opportunities, the Coleman River Scenic Area, and the Southern Nantahala Wilderness.

Tate Branch spreads all but five of its sites on a densely forested loop. Thickets of rhododendron and young hemlock produce secluded campsites. A campground host occupies the first site in the loop, next to the pay station, during the warm season. Seven sites lie by the Tallulah River, running about 30 feet wide at this juncture. The next five sites are between the loop and Forest Service Road 70, which could be a little noisy from the sporadic traffic. Two very shady sites sit inside the loop, along with two low-volume flush toilets and an old-fashioned water pump. One site is located right off FS 70.

What makes this campground different are the sites in a pine forest across FS 70. Just beyond a small parking area are four tent-only campsites. Though not that far from the primary campground, the four sites put like-minded tent campers together. Two of the sites lie fairly close to the road, thus requiring very little walking. However, the other two sites sit a little

CAMPGROUND RATINGS

Beauty: ★★★★★
Site privacy: ★★★★
Site spaciousness: ★★★★★
Quiet: ★★★
Security: ★★★★
Cleanliness/upkeep: ★★★★

Enjoy streamside camping and wilderness hiking deep in the North Georgia mountains.

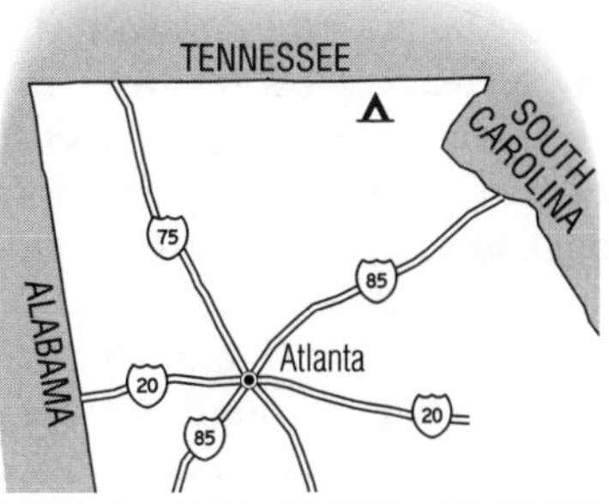

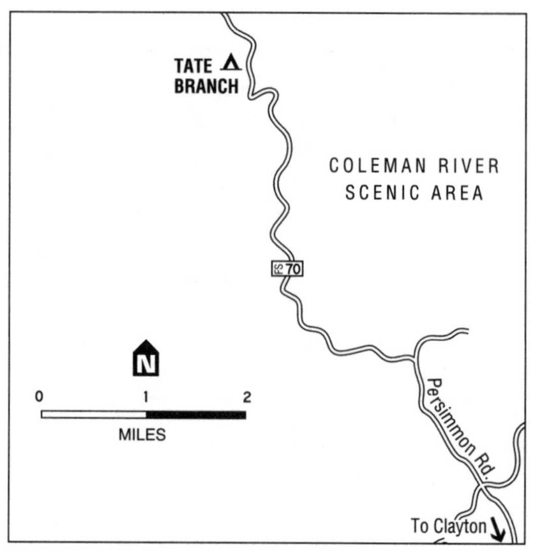

farther back and provide added seclusion. A wildlife opening lies between Tate Branch and the farthest site.

I stayed at the farthest tent-only site on a day that saw thunderstorms saturate the region. Light from the wildlife opening provided a cheery atmosphere. Yet I didn't stay in my tent and sulk. I donned my rain suit, grabbed a fishing pole, and headed for the Coleman River Scenic Area back down FS 70. This 330-acre slice of the past is a remnant of the vast, old-growth forest that once cloaked the length and breadth of the Southern Appalachians. I cast my lure into emerald pools below cascades that tumbled beneath giant boulders. I had no luck with the fish, but I wasn't paying that much attention as I walked along the Coleman River Trail; I was in awe of the huge hemlocks and white pines overhead. Drops of rain descended from branch to branch far above me, only to land on the ferns and rhododendron below. The trail dead-ended after a mile. So I turned around and took it all in from a different perspective.

The Tallulah River rose and turned murky after the storm. I drove along its lower reaches on the way to Clayton. I watched the river froth and boil between sizable boulders as fishermen hoped the "stockers" would take their bait offerings. Tallulah River is stocked with trout weekly during the summer. Back at camp, I mustered a fire from wet wood and warmed my bones as fog crept down the river valley.

The Southern Nantahala Wilderness makes for good exploration also, because it is a rough, rugged, undeveloped area that straddles the North

Carolina–Georgia border. This is a great place to hone your orientation skills by exploring old logging roads and unmaintained trails. However, two marked trails will provide a great hike from known position to known position—they also include great scenery. Get the Southern Nantahala Wilderness map at the Ranger Station in Clayton.

Continue up FS 70 until it crosses into North Carolina. FS 70 turns into FS 56 when it enters the Tar Heel State. Shortly after you cross the border, the Beech Creek Trail (#378) begins on your right. The trail follows Beech Creek through the wilderness to the high country, passing an impressive unnamed falls as it veers toward Case Knife Gap and its high point. Then the trail switchbacks down to FS 56 and the headwaters of the Tallulah River. Take a short road walk back to your vehicle.

At the end of FS 56 is the Deep Gap Branch Trail (#377). It leads 2 miles up the Appalachian Trail at Deep Gap. Just after you enter the wilderness, a short trail leads up a side branch at a falls. Check it out and return to #377. Head east on the AT and come to the Standing Indian shelter at .8 mile. Just 2 miles farther is the top of Standing Indian Mountain. To the east are the headwaters of the Nantahala River and to the west are the headwaters of the Tallulah River. From 5,499 feet, you can look into the Tallulah River gorge. Somewhere down there is Tate Branch Campground. After this hike, you'll be glad to call it home.

To get there, take U.S. 76 west from Clayton for 8 miles. Turn right on Persimmon Road and follow it for 4 miles. Turn left on FS 70 for 4 miles. Tate Branch Campground will be on your left.

KEY INFORMATION

Tate Branch Campground
825 Highway 441 South, P.O. Box 438
Clayton, GA 30525

Operated by: U.S. Forest Service

Information: (706) 782-3320

Open: Year-round

Individual sites: 19

Each site has: Tent pad, fire grate, lantern post, picnic table

Site assignment: First come, first served; no reservations

Registration: Self-registration on site

Facilities: Water pump, low-volume flush toilets

Parking: At campsites only

Fee: $8 per night

Elevation: 2,300 feet

Restrictions:

Pets—On leash only

Fires—In fire grates only

Alcoholic beverages—At campsites only

Vehicles—22-foot trailer length limit

Other—14-day stay limit

UPPER CHATTAHOOCHEE CAMPGROUND

Cleveland, Georgia

Upper Chattahoochee is the newest campground in the Chattahoochee National Forest. And it seems the Forest Service has used all the positive things it has learned in the past to construct this campground. It is located in a long, level cove where the headwaters of the Chattahoochee River merge beneath the high ridges that form the northern border of the Chattahoochee River Basin. Georgia's most famous river flows beyond this campground southward through the state and on to the Gulf of Mexico. Here, deep in the mountains, the Forest Service has integrated the campground into the natural stage of wood, water, and wildlife openings, edged on three sides by the Mark Trail Wilderness.

The attractive campsites stretch out in linear fashion in three sections along a dead-end gravel road. The first group of sites sits in an open flat between the Chattahoochee River and Henson Creek. The second group's sites are dispersed on a short loop along Henson Creek. The third and largest section of sites is at the head of the cove. This arrangement produces a small campground atmosphere, even though it has 34 units.

You can choose whatever woodland setting you please. Some sites are located in open grassy areas. Eight sites are nestled beneath shady hemlocks and require a short walk. But no matter what site you

CAMPGROUND RATINGS

Beauty:	★★★★
Site privacy:	★★★
Site spaciousness:	★★★★★
Quiet:	★★★★★
Security:	★★★★
Cleanliness/upkeep:	★★★★

Camp beside the headwaters of Georgia's most celebrated river, the Chattahoochee.

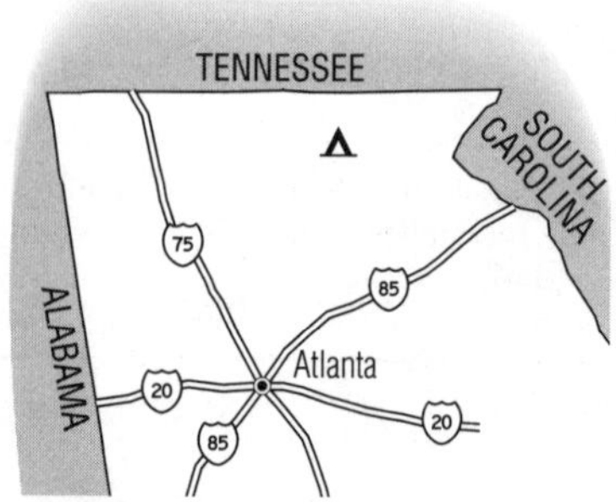

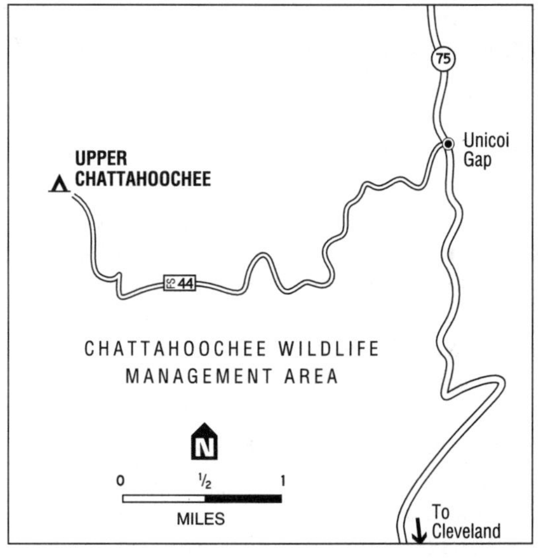

choose, you are never far from the river or one of its feeder streams. Some sites even have a stand-up grill ready for charcoal and your favorite food. Simply put, there is not a bad site in this new campground, only a variety of sites. The five, rough miles of gravel road keep this campground from being overrun. I was the only person at the whole campground during my mid-May stay.

Three bathroom facilities with multiple low-volume flush toilets are adequately distributed, as are the three combination hand-pump water fountain / spigots. It's easy to recycle in the many recycling bins about the campground. For your guardianship, a campground host is usually stationed at the heart of the campground.

The short trail to Horse Trough Falls lies at the very head of the campground. The trail leads .1 mile to a viewing platform that looks up at the falls. The cascade expands from 2 to over 30 feet before it gathers again to flow into the Chattahoochee River, just above the campground.

Another popular hike is the 1.6-mile tramp to Poplar Stomp Gap and the Appalachian Trail on old Forest Service Road 44-C. Once on the AT, turn left and hike to the Low Gap shelter. This section of the AT passes through a mature hardwood forest. Mountain bikers will like the 7-mile loop ride around the Jasus Creek watershed. The loop starts 4.6 miles below the campground on gated FS 44-C.

The Chattahoochee River and its many tributaries offer abundant trout fishing. Low Gap Branch and Jasus Creek provide the angler miles of remote wilderness, where you can fish far back in thick forest that is normally trampled only by the wild creatures of the Mark Trail Wilderness.

The highlight of my Upper Chattahoochee River adventure was the 38-mile loop drive along the Russel-Brasstown Scenic Byway that is formed by highways 17, 180, 348, and 356. First, I drove out FS 44 to U.S. 129 over Unicoi Gap and then north to the High Shoals Falls Scenic Area. I hiked a mile to the falls—a series of five drops totaling 300 feet. Afterwards, I drove to Brasstown Bald, Georgia's highest point. I took the half-mile walk to the viewing tower at 4,784 feet. There I was treated to a 360-degree view of the surrounding mountains.

On I drove, along streams and on top of ridges, taking in the scenery. I stopped at Dukes Creek Falls, a 150-foot drop down a sheer granite canyon. Beyond the town of Helen was Anna Ruby Falls. It is a double falls, .4 mile from the trailhead at the confluence of Curtis and York creeks. I then returned to the Upper Chattahoochee Campground thinking that maybe the byway should be called the Falls Byway.

That evening the skies were clear, so after supper I decided to sleep out in the open. Later, I felt a pitter-patter on my face and groggily erected my shelter just in time for a major downpour. The next morning, the Chattahoochee River was roaring beside my camp. I returned to Horse Trough Falls to see a crashing display of white water that wasn't present the day before. As I drove out of the campground that morning, I felt satisfied with my experience. You will too.

KEY INFORMATION

Upper Chattahoochee Campground
P.O. Box 196, Burton Road
Clarkesville, GA 30523

Operated by: U.S. Forest Service

Information: (706) 754-6221

Open: May 1 to November 31

Individual sites: 34

Each site has: Tent pad, fire grate, lantern post, picnic table

Site assignment: First come, first served; no reservations

Registration: Self-registration on site

Facilities: Pumped water, flush toilets

Parking: At campsites

Fee: $7 per night

Elevation: 2,100 feet

Restrictions:

Pets—On leash only

Fires—In fire rings only

Alcoholic beverages—At campsites only

Vehicles—22-foot trailer length limit

Other—14-day stay limit

To get there, from Cleveland take GA 75 for 17 miles. Then turn left on FS 44 for 5 miles. Upper Chattahoochee Campground will be on your right.

GEORGIA

WILDCAT CAMPGROUND

Clarkesville, Georgia

Wildcat Campground is actually two rough and rustic areas located in the 12,600-acre Lake Burton Wildlife Management Area, contiguous to the Tray Mountain Wilderness. A single-lane road with turnouts traces Wildcat Creek and all but eliminates RVs from entering the area. The Forest Service banished roadside camping along Wildcat Creek and constructed these campgrounds to concentrate human impact into two areas. The Lake Burton Wildlife Management Area is lightly used except during hunting season.

The two campgrounds are spartan and will put you in the mood for outdoor recreation. Both areas have low-flow flush toilets and recycling bins. You must get your water from the creek. Be sure to treat or boil it before consuming.

Wildcat Area #1 is located just above the confluence of Wildcat Creek and Jessie Branch. Most of the 16 sites are pinched on either side of a loop road circling a creekside flat. However, a few sites rest outside the loop and require a short walk uphill, offering more seclusion and space. Big trees are scattered around the campground, providing ample shade and making up for minimal groundcover. An interesting feature of the campground is the abundance of large rocks placed about the campground by the Forest Service for aesthetics and site delineation. They also make good seats and great tables.

CAMPGROUND RATINGS

Beauty:	★★★★★
Site privacy:	★★★
Site spaciousness:	★★★
Quiet:	★★★★
Security:	★★★
Cleanliness/upkeep:	★★★★

Wildlife, water, and wilderness are only a trail away at Wildcat Campground.

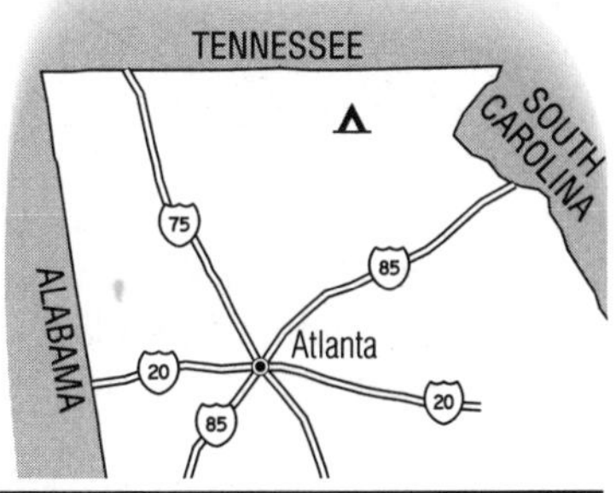

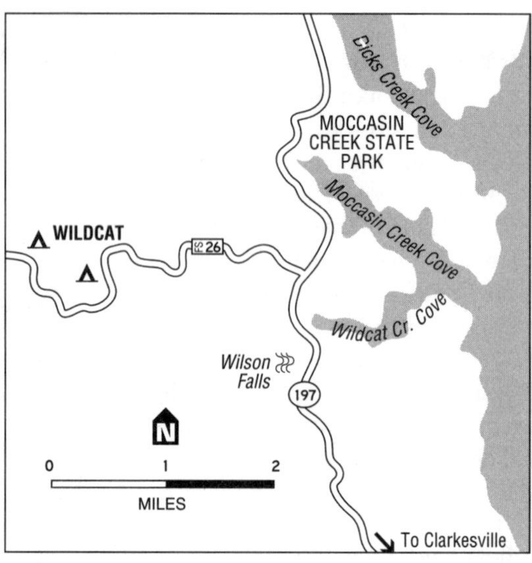

Wildcat Area #2 is bigger and, in my opinion, the better of the two. It has 16 campsites arranged along a figure-eight creekside loop. Large rocks are even more abundant here beneath the tall forest. In addition, the campsites here are larger than at Wildcat Area #1. A grassy field created by the Forest Service as a wildlife opening is adjacent to the campground, providing a good escape should you feel closed in by the forest. Just across the creek is the Tray Mountain Wilderness boundary.

For water fun, try fishing, swimming, and boating. Wildcat Creek is stocked weekly during the summer with trout from the Lake Burton Hatchery. Forest Service Road 26 provides easy access to good pools as well as the Sliding Rock, a popular swimming hole where you can skim over a slippery rock into a cool mountain stream. Be careful, though; those rocks *are* slippery. The slide is visible from FS 26 before you reach the campgrounds. For true backwoods fishing, follow Wildcat Creek into the wilderness and away from the road. Nearby Lake Burton provides other watery recreation opportunities if you own or want to rent a boat.

No trails start from the campgrounds, but you'll find plenty nearby. Just up FS 26 are the Bramlett Ridge and Pigpen Ridge trails. Bramlett Ridge Trail leads 2 miles into the heart of the Tray Mountain Wilderness intersecting the Appalachian Trail at Round Top. Follow the AT north and you can loop back to your car from Addis Gap. The Pigpen Ridge Trail leads east 2 miles to Moccasin Creek and a series of waterfalls and slides. You can also access the

Moccasin Creek Trail from Moccasin Creek State Park at Lake Burton.

Moccasin Creek is a gem of a trail. It combines scenic beauty with man-made wildlife openings, enabling you to see the Forest Service's efforts to create a better habitat for the region's fauna. Wildlife openings are man-made clearings containing highly nutritional plants and grasses that are sown for birds, turkey, deer, and other animals. Forest and grassland interface in these openings, producing "edges" where a greater variety of food plants from both environments mix to attract wildlife. Wildlife management is a key element of the Forest Service's multiple-use concept for our national forests.

Other trails with wildlife openings, such as North Fork Trail, Parks Gap Trail, and old Deep Gap Road, connect with the Moccasin Creek Trail forming wildlife viewing loops. The side trails are rarely used during the summer and can provide an isolated wildlife hiking experience. Get the Lake Burton Wildlife Management Area map from the Moccasin Creek State Park office.

Kastner's Store is located just south of FS 26 on GA 197 if you need supplies. Other services can be accessed along this road as well. Wildcat is an appropriate name for this campground in the middle of a wildlife management area.

To get there, take GA 197 north from Clarkesville for 22 miles. Turn left up a steep hill on FS 26. Follow FS 26 for 3 miles to Wildcat Camping Area #1; it will be on your right. Wildcat Camping Area #2 is 1 mile farther, also on your right.

KEY INFORMATION

Wildcat Campground
825 Highway 441 South, P.O. Box 438
Clayton, GA 30525

Operated by: U.S. Forest Service

Information: (706) 782-3320

Open: Year-round

Individual sites: Area #1: 16; Area #2: 16

Each site has: Tent pad, lantern post, fire pit, picnic table

Site assignment: First come, first served; no reservations

Registration: Self-registration on site

Facilities: Low-volume flush toilets

Parking: At campsites only

Fee: $5 per night

Elevation: Area #1: 2,100 feet; Area #2: 2,400 feet

Restrictions:

Pets—On leash only

Fires—In fire rings only

Alcoholic beverages—At campsites only

Vehicles—22-foot trailer length limit

Other—14-day stay limit

APPENDICES

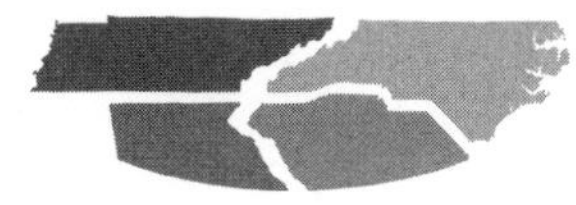

APPENDIX A
Camping Equipment Checklist

Except for the large and bulky items on this list, I keep a plastic storage container full of the essentials of car camping so that they're ready to go when I am. I make a last-minute check of the inventory, resupply anything that's low or missing, and away I go!

Cooking Utensils
Bottle opener
Bottles of salt, pepper, spices, sugar, cooking oil, and maple syrup in waterproof, spill-proof containers
Can opener
Cups, plastic or tin
Dish soap (biodegradable), sponge, and towel
Flatware
Food of your choice
Frying pan
Fuel for stove
Matches in waterproof container
Plates
Pocketknife
Pot with lid
Spatula
Stove
Tin foil
Wooden spoon

First Aid Kit
Band-Aids
First aid cream
Gauze pads
Ibuprofen or aspirin
Insect repellent
Moleskin
Snakebite kit
Sunscreen / chapstick
Tape, waterproof adhesive

Sleeping Gear
Pillow
Sleeping bag
Sleeping pad, inflatable or insulated
Tent with ground tarp and rainfly

Miscellaneous
Bath soap (biodegradable), washcloth, and towel
Camp chair
Candles
Cooler
Deck of cards
Fire starter
Flashlight with fresh batteries
Foul weather clothing
Maps (road, topographic, trails, etc.)
Paper towels
Plastic zip-top bags
Sunglasses
Toilet paper
Water bottle
Wool blanket

Optional
Barbecue grill
Binoculars
Books on bird, plant, and wildlife identification
Fishing rod and tackle
Hatchet
Lantern

APPENDIX B
Information

Chattahoochee National Forest
1755 Cleveland Highway
Gainesville, GA 30501
(770) 536-0541

Cherokee National Forest
2800 N. Ocoee Street
P.O. Box 2010
Cleveland, TN 37311
(423) 476-9700

Georgia State Parks
205 Butler Street, Suite 1352 East
Atlanta, GA 30334
(404) 656-3530

North Carolina State Parks
P.O. Box 27687
Raleigh, NC 27611-7687
(919) 733-4181

Pisgah & Nantahala National Forests
P.O. Box 2750
Asheville, NC 28802
(704) 257-4200

South Carolina State Parks
1205 Pendleton Street
Columbia, SC 29201
(803) 734-0156

Sumter National Forest
4931 Broad River Road
Columbia, SC 29210-4021
(803) 561-4000

Tennessee State Parks
401 Church Street
LNC Tower, 7th Floor
Nashville, TN 37243
(888) 867-2757

APPENDIX C
Suggested Reading and Reference

Appalachian Trail Guide to Tennessee-North Carolina. Edgar, Kevin. Appalachian Trail Conference, 1992.

Day & Overnight Hikes in the Great Smoky Mountains National Park. Molloy, Johnny. Menasha Ridge Press, 1995.

Great Smoky Mountains. Houk, Rose. Houghton Mifflin, 1993.

Hiking South Carolina Trails. de Hart, Allen. The Globe Pequot Press, 1994.

Hiking Trails of Joyce Kilmer and Citico Creek Wilderness Areas. Homan, Tim. Peachtree Publishers, Ltd., 1990.

The Hiking Trails of North Georgia. Homan, Tim. Peachtree Publishers, Ltd., 1987.

Hiking Trails of the Smokies. Kemp, Steve, editor. Great Smoky Mountains Natural History Association, 1994.

Natural Wonders of Tennessee. Lawrence, Ardi & H. Lea. Country Roads Press, 1994.

North Carolina Hiking Trails. de Hart, Allen. Appalachian Mountain Club Books, 1988.

Our Southern Highlanders. Kephart, Horace. University of Tennessee Press, 1984.

Smoky Mountain Hiking & Camping. Barnes, Lee. Menasha Ridge Press, 1994.

Strangers in High Places. Frome, Michael. University of Tennessee Press, 1994.

Trees of the Smokies. Kemp, Steve. Great Smoky Mountains Natural History Association, 1993.

Trial By Trail: Backpacking in the Smoky Mountains. Molloy, Johnny. University of Tennessee Press, 1996.

The Unofficial Guide to the Great Smoky and Blue Ridge Mountains. Sehlinger, Bob & Surkiewicz, Joe. Macmillan, 1997.

Wilderness Trails of Tennessee's Cherokee National Forest. Skelton, Will, editor. University of Tennessee Press, 1992.

ABOUT THE AUTHOR

A native Tennessean, Johnny Molloy was born in Memphis and moved to Knoxville in 1980 to attend the University of Tennessee. It was there, on a backpacking foray into the Great Smoky Mountains National Park, that he developed a love of the natural world—a love that has become the primary focus of his life.

Though a disaster, that trip unleashed a passion for the outdoors that has encompassed more than 1200 nights in the wild over the past 12 years. He has spent over 650 nights in the Smokies alone, cultivating his woodmanship and expertise on those lofty mountains. He has completed his fourth year as a GSMNP adopt-a-trail volunteer and currently maintains Little Bottoms Trail.

After graduating from the University of Tennessee in 1987 and continuing to spend ever-increasing time in natural places, he became more skilled in a variety of environments. Upon suggestion and encouragement from friends, he began to parlay his skill into an occupation. The results of his efforts are three books: *Day & Overnight Hikes in the Great Smoky Mountains National Park* (Menasha Ridge Press, 1995); *Trial by Trail: Backpacking in the Smoky Mountains* (University of Tennessee Press, 1996); and *The Best in Tent Camping: Smoky Mountains* (Menasha Ridge Press, 1997). In addition, he has authored numerous magazine articles.

Today, Johnny continues to write about, and travel extensively to, all four corners of the United States indulging in a variety of outdoor pursuits. He is currently writing a book about a summer in the West entitled *West by Southeast,* as well as another book for Menasha Ridge Press entitled *The Best in Tent Camping: Florida.*